Jacques Ellul on Violence, Resistance, and War

Jacques Ellul on Violence, Resistance, and War

EDITED BY

Jeffrey M. Shaw

&

Timothy J. Demy

PICKWICK *Publications* · Eugene, Oregon

JACQUES ELLUL ON VIOLENCE, RESISTANCE, AND WAR

Pickwick Publications
An Imprint of Wipf and Stock Publishers
199 W. 8th Ave., Suite 3
Eugene, OR 97401

www.wipfandstock.com

PAPERBACK ISBN: 978-1-4982-7888-1
HARDCOVER ISBN: 978-1-4982-7890-4

Cataloguing-in-Publication data:

Jacques Ellul on violence, resistance, and war / edited by Jeffrey M. Shaw
    and Timothy J. Demy.

    xvi + 172 pp. ; 23 cm. Includes bibliographical references and index(es).

    ISBN 978-1-4982-7888-1 (paperback) | ISBN 978-1-4982-7890-4 (hardback)

    1. Ellul, Jacques, 1912–1994—Political and social views. 2. Violence—Religious aspects—Christianity. I. Shaw, Jeffrey M. II. Demy, Timothy J. III. Title.

BX4827.E5 J3 2016

Manufactured in the U.S.A.   04/08/16

Disclaimer: The views expressed in this book are solely those of the individual authors and do not reflect the views of the Naval War College of any other governmental organization.

Contents

Acknowledgments

THERE ARE MANY PEOPLE who helped put this book together, whether providing encouragement, or in formulating the idea to actually publish a book on Jacques Ellul and war. First among these is Tim Demy, friend and colleague at the Naval War College, and co-editor of this volume. It was his idea to bring together the leading scholars studying Ellul and those continuing to apply Ellul's methodology in the twenty-first century. It is thanks to him that this book is in print.

Few books on Ellul see the light of day without David Gill's active involvement. President of the International Jacques Ellul Society, David not only encouraged the project, but gave me permission to use articles that had previously been published in the Ellul Forum over the years. By doing so, readers can now reference articles on the topic of Ellul and war in a single volume.

Christian Amondson at Wipf and Stock has, as always, provided helpful oversight of this project, along with Brian Palmer, Laura Poncy, Ted Lewis, Joshua Little, and Calvin Jaffarian. Thanks are also due to the entire Wipf and Stock team, to include copy editors, cover designers, marketers, and contracting personnel.

Other Ellul scholars, friends, and colleagues who helped bring this volume to print include Lisa Richmond, who diligently reviewed and provided editing and stylistic suggestions for some of the following chapters. Thanks also to Allyson Rogers, Kent Walker, Bernard Bouyssou, Jerome Ellul, Sylvie Justome, Pierre Castro, and especially Daniel and Anita Cerezuelle for their hospitality and conversation as hosts to visiting Ellulians in the summer of 2015.

Contributors

Andy Alexis-Baker holds a PhD in theology from Marquette University and teaches theology and religious studies at Arrupe College at Loyola University Chicago. He is co-editor of *A Faith Embracing All Creatures: Addressing Commonly Asked Questions about Christian Care for Animals* (2012) and *A Faith Encompassing All Creation: Addressing Commonly Asked Questions about Christian Care for the Environment* (2014) in the Peaceable Kingdom series with Cascade Books. His current research is on Christian theology and nonhuman animals.

Stanley Uche Anozie holds a philosophy teaching position at Sacred Heart College of Peterborough, Ontario, Canada. He had his Bachelors of Philosophy and Theology at Seat of Wisdom Seminary Nigeria, an affiliate institute of Pontifical Urban University, Rome. He obtained his PhD from the Dominican University College of Philosophy and Theology in Ottawa, Canada. Anozie has written some selected published works: "The Impact of Christianity in African Development so far" in *Africa and the Challenges of the 21st Century* (Enwisdomization Journal, 2001), "Human Rights and Terrorism: Nigeria-Niger Delta Oil War" in *Morality and Terrorism* (Nortia Press, 2012), and *Aristotle's Phronesis: an influence on Gadamer's Hermeneutical Circle and Philosophical Hermeneutics* (Brill Publishers, forthcoming). Anozie is an International Editorial and Advisory Board Member of Alternative Perspectives and Global Concerns (APGC), a Scholarly Organization based in Ottawa, Canada. He is also a member of American Philosophical Association (APA, Eastern Division).

Mark D. Baker is professor of mission and theology at Fresno Pacific Biblical Seminary. He was a missionary in Honduras for ten years. He has authored books in Spanish and English, including *Religious No More: Building Communities of Grace and Freedom* which utilizes Ellul's work. While completing his M.A. at New College Berkeley he studied Ellul with David Gill and Vernard Eller and he completed a PhD in theology and ethics at Duke University.

Timothy J. Demy is Professor of Military Ethics at the US Naval War College. Prior to his faculty appointment at the Naval War College, he served as a Navy chaplain for 27 years holding assignments afloat and ashore with the Navy, Marine Corps, and Coast Guard. He received a ThD in historical theology from Dallas Theological Seminary and a PhD in Humanities from Salve Regina University. He also completed the Master of Studies in international relations from the University of Cambridge and the Master of Arts in National Security and Strategic Studies from the Naval War College. He is the author and editor of numerous articles and books on a variety of historical, ethical, and theological subjects. He also serves as the American managing editor of the *Journal of Military Ethics*.

Peter K. Fallon is Professor of Media Studies at Roosevelt University. He is the author of three books; *Printing, Literacy, and Education in Eighteenth Century Ireland: Why the Irish Speak English* (winner of the Marshall McLuhan Award for Outstanding Book in 2007), *The Metaphysics of Media: Toward an End to Postmodern Cynicism and the Construction of a Virtuous Reality* (winner of the Lewis Mumford Award for Outstanding Scholarship in Technology, 2010), and *Cultural Defiance, Cultural Deviance*. A former editor (2009–11) of *EME: Explorations in Media Ecology*, the international scholarly journal of the Media Ecology Association, Fallon serves on the editorial board of *Second Nature*, an online journal for critical study of technology and new media from a Christian perspective.

David Gill wrote his PhD dissertation on "The Word of God in the Ethics of Jacques Ellul" at the University of Southern California and has published countless reviews, essays, comments, and book notes on Ellul over the past forty years. He is founding president (2000) of the International Jacques Ellul Society and after a forty year career as professor of business ethics and theological ethics is now a writer based in Berkeley/Oakland, California.

Andrew Goddard is a Senior Research Fellow of the Kirby Laing Institute of Christian Ethics, Cambridge, UK. He did his doctorate on Jacques Ellul, which was published as *Living the Word, Resisting the World* (Paternoster, 2003) and is a director of the International Jacques Ellul Society.

Dal Yong Jin finished his PhD degree from the Institute of Communications Research at the University of Illinois at Urbana Champaign. His major research and teaching interests are on social media and convergence, mobile technologies and game studies, globalization and media, transnational cultural studies, and the political economy of media and culture. He is the author of several books, such as *New Korean Wave: Transnational Cultural Power in the Age of Social Media* (University of Illinois Press, in press 2015), and *Digital Platforms, Imperialism and Political Culture* (Routledge, 2015). He has also edited two books, including *Global Media Convergence and Cultural Transformation: Emerging Social Patterns and Characteristics* (IGI Global, 2011) and *The Political Economies of Media: the Transformation of the Global Media Industries* (Bloomsbury, 2011).

Richard L. Kirkpatrick attended Connecticut College and The Johns Hopkins University. He studied Ellul and Machiavelli under the guidance of Professor F. Edward Cranz, author of *Nicholas of Cusa and the Renaissance*, and other works. This piece is dedicated to him.

David Lovekin is Professor of Philosophy Emeritus at Hastings College, Hastings, Nebraska. He is the author of *Technique, Discourse, and Consciousness: An Introduction to the Philosophy of Jacques Ellul* and editor with Donald Phillip Verene of *Essays in Humanity and Technology*. He is co-translator of Jacques Ellul's *The Empire of Non-Sense*. He has published numerous essays on Ellul and Giambattista Vico that deal with technology as a problem for the philosophy of culture in the spirit of Ernst Cassirer with the idea of technology as a symbolic form. His most recent essay is "Looking and Seeing: the Play of Image and Word—the Wager of Art in the Technological Society." He is contributing editor of *The Ellul Forum* and serves as a member of the International Jacques Ellul Society. He was a recipient of five grants from the National Endowment for the Humanities. His photography has been published in numerous books and periodicals; his most recent work appears on covers of the *Prairie Schooner,* the literary magazine of the University of Nebraska, Lincoln, and in the Modern Arts/Midwest, Midtown gallery in Omaha, Nebraska.

Randal Marlin is currently Adjunct Research Professor in the Department of Philosophy at Carleton University in Ottawa, Canada, having retired from full-time teaching in 2001. He has degrees in philosophy from Princeton, McGill, and Toronto (Ph.D.), and studied with Jacques Ellul during a sabbatical in Bordeaux in 1979–80, assisted by a Canadian Department of Defence Fellowship. His publications include *Propaganda and the Ethics of Persuasion* (Broadview Press, second edition, 2013) and numerous articles and reviews. Vice-President of the *IJES*, he organized an international conference on Ellul in Ottawa, July, 2014, jointly with Dominican University College.

Jeffrey M. Shaw is an Associate Professor of Strategy and Policy at the US Naval War College. He is the author of *Illusions of Freedom: Thomas Merton and Jacques Ellul on Technology and the Human Condition* (Wipf and Stock, 2014). He is also co-editor of the forthcoming 3-volume *Wars of Religion: An Encyclopedia of Faith and Conflict* with Dr. Timothy J. Demy and is a co-author of the forthcoming *The Reformers on War, Peace, and Justice: A Survey,* from Wipf and Stock. His book chapters include "The Ogaden War" in *Peripheries of the Cold War* (Verlag Koningshausen & Neumann, September, 2015) and "War and Technology: Precision, Nanotechnology, and Globalization" in *The Means to Kill - Essays on the Interdependence of War and Technology from Ancient Rome to the Age of Drones,* forthcoming from McFarland. He holds a PhD in Humanities from Salve Regina University in Newport, RI.

David Stokes is an assistant professor of theology at Providence College. He holds a BA from the University of the South (Sewanee), an MA from Keble College Oxford, and a PhD from the Princeton Theological Seminary. For thirty years as an Anglican priest he has served parishes both in England and the United States. Presently he is a retired Roman Catholic priest. His primary interests are the theology of Karl Barth, the thought of Sören Kierkegaard, and the development of biblical hermeneutics.

Introduction

It is nearly impossible to read the news and not stumble across a headline that proclaims some act of violence somewhere in the world. Whether conflict between nations, civil wars, or some combination of both, the twenty-first century has seen no decrease in war, terrorism, and bloodshed. Why is this? Has not our inter-connected and globalized world learned yet to live peacefully?

While some philosophers and academics have proclaimed that today's world is actually more peaceful and less violent than in ages past, it would be difficult to argue that acts of sensational and purposeful violence have not captivated us over the last few decades. There is, however, one voice among many that has given us plenty to think about regarding some of the pitfalls that our increasingly technological world may continue to face. Jacques Ellul is that voice. This book brings together a number of perspectives on Ellul's thinking about violence and war. Collected from conference presentations, previous editions of the *Ellul Forum*, or just plain new thinking, these articles give the reader an overview of Ellul's writing on violence, resistance, and war.

It is always important to keep in mind when reading Ellul that he is not a traditional philosopher. Rather than presenting a series of answers to various questions, his dialectical method provokes, prods, and compels us to think more deeply about the human condition as we find it. This book presents eleven chapters that address the topic of violence, resistance, and war in Ellul's thinking.

David Gill leads off with a general overview of Ellul on violence. This chapter provides some background and framework for those that follow.

David Stokes then presents a comparison of Ellul with John Calvin and Karl Barth. Andrew Goddard brings us an updated version of Ellul and the just war tradition. Dal Yon Jing offers an Ellulian methodology for examining the consequences of increased cyber surveillance and security, highlighting some of the pitfalls inherent in an increasingly technological world. Stanley Anozie looks at the Nigerian government's war against Boko Haram through the lens of Ellul's thinking on war and propaganda. Andy Alexis-Baker looks at "just policing," using Ellul as a backdrop. Richard Kirkpatrick presents a new analysis of Ellul and Machiavelli. Jeff Shaw examines Ellul and Thomas Merton and their thinking on propaganda as a form of violence. Peter Fallon looks at propaganda as well, but as a form of psychic violence. David Lovekin writes on technology and perpetual war, and Mark Baker concludes the chapters with his assessment of how Ellul influenced him to become a Christian pacifist. There are two book reviews in the appendix to help acquaint (or reacquaint, as the case may be) readers with Ellul's thinking on violence.

Throughout the book, readers may encounter the word *technique*. Anyone familiar with Ellul and his writing will instantly recognize this concept—it is simply the focal point of his entire argument from his magnum opus *The Technological Society*. In order to bring new readers into the fold, according to Ellul,

> *Technique* refers to any complex of standardized means for attaining a predetermined result. Thus, it converts spontaneous and unreflective behavior into behavior that is deliberate and rationalized. The Technical Man is fascinated by results, by the immediate consequences of setting standardized devices into motion. He cannot help admiring the spectacular effectiveness of nuclear weapons of war. Above all, he is committed to the "one best way" to achieve any designated objective.[1]

Technique is a key concept that one must understand in order to grasp Ellul's message. It is a concept that will appear frequently in any discussion of Ellul.

Jacques Ellul does not belong to either the left or the right; he is neither liberal nor conservative. Only his individual positions on any given topic can be classified as such, and even then, it is difficult to locate him in any particular camp. This may be due to the fact that his thinking emerges from mid-twentieth century France, and is generally far more sophisticated than

---

1. Ellul, *Technological Society,* vi.

what we might find in early twenty-first century America. What passes for informed debate today is often no more than intellectual dribble, whether we get it from Jon Stewart or Rush Limbaugh. The parameters of discourse have collapsed to such a degree that we often find it difficult to entertain ideas that do not meet our predetermined specifications. Many who have read and considered Ellul's work do not agree with his stance—something which you will find in the pages ahead. Ellul was not looking for followers, nor was he trying to convince anyone to think like he did. He simply presented his thinking to the world, and invited others to think for themselves, whether by using his writing as a starting point or not.

Thus, Ellul can be difficult for readers who are expecting to pick up a book that helps reinforce their particular stereotypes. If you want a book that supports your preconceptions about the way you think the world really is, stop reading now. If, however, you want to critically examine ideas of importance, and encounter ideas that may not necessarily be ones with which you thoroughly agree, then continue on, and join in the debate with Ellul, the scholar from Bordeaux, and the ideas that he has inspired in those who have interacted with his work. Better yet, take a look online at the Ellul Forum (https://journals.wheaton.edu/index.php/ellul) and perhaps contribute something to the discussion. And finally, peruse the large selection of Ellul's work that has been translated by Wipf and Stock, and begin the journey into Ellul's sociological and theological thinking. You will not be disappointed!

References

Ellul, Jacques. *The Technological Society*. Translated by John Wilkerson. New York: Vintage, 1964.

Chapter 1

Jacques Ellul on Living in a Violent World[1]

David Gill

THE ENGLISH VERSION OF Jacques Ellul's book, *Violence: Reflections from a Christian Perspective,* was first published in 1969. Such was the intense interest in Ellul's thought in that time period that the English translation was actually published three years in advance of the French original which was titled *Contre les violents,* literally "against the violent" or "against violence," which is a bit stronger title than "reflections on violence." Forty years later, is it possible to discern any measurable impact of Ellul's essay on the level of violence in our world? I don't think so, since it's worse than ever. And is it possible forty years later to discern any significant impact of Ellul's essay on the way Christians in the Francophone or Anglophone worlds view violence? Again, I don't think so. The militaristic and violent attitudes of many Christians today are shocking, to say the least. The words embarrassing, dangerous, ignorant, faithless, and worldly are some of the other terms that come to mind. Other "religious" peoples have certainly also exhibited penchants for violence, the severity of which Ellul could scarcely have imagined. Of course, this is not Ellul's fault—except in the sense that he might have written more clearly and persuasively, but this is a charge that could be leveled at many great thinkers in our field and in many other fields as well.

1. This chapter is derived from a presentation delivered at the Society of Christian Ethics Annual Meeting, Washington, DC, January 7, 2012.

In this centenary year of Jacques Ellul's birth (January 6, 1912—May 19, 1994) I am among those suggesting that the twentieth-century polymath of Bordeaux deserves a renewed and serious hearing in our troubled twenty-first century. Certainly on topics such as technology, politics, communications, religion, and ethics such attention is warranted. But on the specific problem of violence he has a great deal to say to us as well. Two preliminary ideas will set the stage for a discussion of his views on violence.

The first preliminary has to do with the context in which and from which Ellul wrote about violence. His childhood unfolded in France during the Great War which embroiled France and all of Europe. The Russian Revolution occurred when he was seven years old and loomed over Europe much more intensely than it did a distant USA. From 1936 to 1939 Ellul and many of his friends were close observers and in some cases actual participants in the Spanish Civil War (Bordeaux lies not far north of the Spanish border). During the Second World War, Nazi Germany occupied France, including Bordeaux in the Southwest. Ellul was fired from his university post for disloyalty to the collaborating Vichy government and spent the next four years of the occupation living and working on a farm outside of Bordeaux and as an active participant/leader in the Resistance. He says he did not personally engage in violence against the German forces but he knew of their activity rounding up the local Jewish population and sending them off to Auschwitz. His own elderly father was arrested and sent to a prison near the Swiss border where he became ill and died within a year. Ellul and his friends helped to hide Jewish men and women and provide them with false identity papers. In the 1950s, Ellul was among those urging the early decolonization of Algeria to avoid bloodshed. Their voices were ignored with horrible, violent consequences. And in the West itself after 1945, Ellul often decried the triumph of the spirit and weapons of war over the victors themselves, not just over the vanquished. Finally, on the local level, Ellul was for many years in the fifties and sixties a leader in a local juvenile gang "prevention club," working with street gang members and their families to help them find another way, often also acting as their legal advocate in courtroom settings. During the 1968 French university student strikes and the violence which followed, Ellul was a faculty sympathizer and student advocate. There is no need to review the world situation from the sixties to the nineties since it is so well known. But it is important to understand that when Ellul writes about violence, he is anything but an ivory tower theorist unfamiliar with actual conflict.

The second preliminary note has to do with Ellul's vocation as an intellectual and how this relates to our understanding of his writings on violence or any other topic. In short, Ellul is a prophet, a dialectician, and an existentialist. Expecting him to be anything else will lead to great misunderstanding and disappointment. He is a *prophet* rather than a teacher in the sense that he brings a specific message, a word, from outside a given topic or situation that can illuminate something that has been missing or overlooked. He upsets and challenges conventions and assumptions and standard ways of thinking and seeing. He is strange and uncomfortable. He is not the systematic, constructive teacher but the troubling critic. He is a *dialectician* in that he fundamentally believes that we understand reality by grasping the simultaneous truth of what appear to be opposites and contradictions, paradoxes, anomalies. This is for Ellul as fundamental to the Bible and theology as it is to sociology and history. Thus, Jesus is divine and human, God is three and one, the state is Babylon and Jerusalem, violence is necessary and unacceptable. There is no resolution of such dialectic intellectually or rationally—the resolution, or the synthesis, happens in life, in being and in acting. In other words we can *live* with the contradictions of violence, theology, etc., but we cannot iron them out in our theories and explanations. And this is where the *existentialist* label comes in. Ellul is an heir of Sōren Kierkegaard. He is relentlessly anti-Modern. He cares nothing for comprehensive systems and theories and everything for life at this moment in this context. All of this may be unsatisfying to readers of Ellul who want something other than what he has to give. But what Ellul has to offer if taken for what it is, is a great gift to our thinking and conversation; it is not an adequate final destination, but a valuable part of the journey.

One other comment on Ellul's approach: in his classic two-volume *Maincurrents in Sociological Thought,* Raymond Aron summarizes a basic difference between the continental European sociologists like Max Weber and Emile Durkheim and those of the American tradition. The continental types tended to create descriptive models, inviting us to reflect on their explanatory power, while the Americans tend to generalize based on statistical, empirical research. This is helpful in understanding Ellul's approach in this and other works. There is a vast research behind his work but it is not statistics so much as history and culture. Readers seeking social scientific research in that quantitative mode will almost always find Ellul frustrating and unpersuasive. With regard to violence, Ellul creates a model to try to explain it; in the old metaphor of shoes and feet, his explanatory model is like a shoe. It is for us to try it on, and to see if it fits as we live out our own reflection and experience, and as we walk in it.

So let me review briefly Ellul's discussion of violence, sticking fairly closely to his 1969 book, *Violence*. Ellul first reviews how he sees the historical traditions in the Christian church—from the virtual pacifism (partly principled, partly by default) of the first three centuries when Christianity was excluded from power to the epoch of Christendom when from St. Augustine to Martin Luther the theologians approved the just use of force and violence internally and just wars externally. He then moves to the post-Christendom world which ranges from the advocates of pacifism and non-violent resistance on the one hand to the theology of revolution on the other and everything in between.

Ellul concludes his review of this history by saying those who seek a Christian theory for the appropriate use of violence

> try to formulate a compromise between the demands of the Christ and the necessities of the world, to work out a quantitative determination, a balance of factors that will bring in a viable social order . . . [they] cherish the hope that the various elements involved can be brought into accord. They forget that this is the world that has absolutely rejected Jesus Christ, that there can be no accord between the values, the bases, the *stoikea* of the world and those of the revelation . . . [T]he attempt to assimilate world and faith to each other is one mistake, and the attempt to separate them radically is another . . . If the Incarnation has a meaning it can only be that God came into the most abominable of places (and he did not, by his coming, either validate or change that place). . . So we must stand at a distance from our society, its tendencies and movements, but we must never break with it, for the Incarnation has taken place. We are invited to take part in a dialectic, to be in the world but not of it, and thus to seek out a particular, a specifically Christian position. It is from this point of view that we shall consider this problem of violence, which is so urgent and tragic today.[2]

Ellul argues that we need much more realism in our understanding of violence. Violence is endemic to human history; it is found everywhere and at all times. In this, Ellul agrees with Thomas Hobbes. This is the state of nature. Theologically, biblical revelation shows the same thing: violence is of the order of the fall; from Cain killing Abel to the world crucifying

2. Ellul, *Violence*, 24–26.

Jesus to the apocalyptic conflict of Armageddon, violence is the condition of humanity. Politically, all states are based on violence and there is no fundamental difference between violence and force.

Even as moral and Christian-influenced a nation as the USA, Ellul argues that free market competition, such as that which supports the US economy, can represent a kind of economic violence and coercion no different than what one would find in a system based on centralized planning. Violence is about coercing and attacking others, forcing their acquiescence, dominating and imposing your will upon them. This can be done physically, of course, but it is still violence if the coercion is psychological, economic, ideological, or otherwise. It is the opposite of inviting or allowing a free choice or response by the other.

Violence, Ellul argues, is the natural condition of humanity; it is part of the order of *necessity*. Some violent acts may seem like they are the free, reckless striking out against others. But whether premeditated and planned or not, violence in its various forms is not about freedom but about necessity. In other words, violence is a kind of interwoven web that draws us into its expression that imposes itself on our lives, that pressures us to participate in it and continue it.

But as hopeless and pessimistic as all of that sounds, necessity is not quite the same thing as fatality or destiny. It is possible to resist. It cannot be eliminated from a fallen world but it is important to try to mitigate its impacts, address and ameliorate where possible the conditions that foment it, and heal and comfort those suffering from it. Ellul has sometimes written that he describes a world that will exist if we do nothing to resist it or refuse its direction. He has said that when God wants someone to do something he first makes him mad. It is only when we feel that a situation is hopeless and completely sealed off that we will sometimes finally act.

But let's go back to violence in the order of necessity. Ellul's views on violence can basically be summarized by the following main points:

1. Continuity: once you start using violence you can't get away from it.

2. Reciprocity: those who live by the sword will die by the sword; using violence against an enemy produces enemies intent on retaliation.

3. Sameness: all violence is the same, of a piece; it is impossible to distinguish justified and unjustified or liberating and enslaving violence; one kind leads to the others, involves the others.

4. Violence begets only violence and violence-corrupted ends: the means affect the character of the end. Violent means do not and cannot produce a peaceful end. At best the result is a kind of "détente-based-on-violence."

5. Justification: all users of violence try to justify it and themselves; but it is always a sign of incapacity, an inability to imagine or follow an alternative path, always from mixed motives that may include hatred, greed, etc.; it leads to hypocrisy.

These five precepts are perhaps overstated, but Ellul has seen too many alleged liberators with clean hands wind up being corrupted by their very process of taking and holding power. He has seen too many idealistic movements turn into violent oppression and too much high-flown rhetoric masking a hidden violence under the surface. Too many wars of liberation end in slavery, and too many "wars to end wars" lead to more and worse wars. So Ellul's bold, overstated, oversimplified descriptions of violence are actually a helpful prophetic challenge: if we get involved in any violence or coercion, we had better do so with our eyes open. If we don't resist, this is all we are left with.

Ellul believes that this violence in the world of necessity is inescapable in any total sense. We are caught in it and there is no total escape from its impact. In practice we will find ourselves in situations where we simply are cornered and cannot find another way out than violence, whether that is killing or maiming an attacker, trying to assassinate a tyrant, joining an army to beat back an invading force, or laying off a band of loyal workers before our company winds up in bankruptcy. We can't find another way. We act in a violent fashion. And for Ellul this is understandable and even "condonable" in some cases. Ellul says that violence can even have its own virtues within this world of necessity: it can bring about disorder, crush the lie, reveal the true situation, and explode the façade. So Ellul condones the violent revolts of at least some oppressed groups. But what he says is that this is not holy or Christian or just violence—but rather is an example of yielding to necessity in a fallen world. The appropriate rhetoric is not "God led me to kill you" but "I just couldn't find another way so I had to kill him."

But for Christians, Ellul says, we must not assume that what is natural is what is good or that what is necessary is legitimate. Christ came to shatter necessity and introduce freedom. Christ makes us free to struggle against necessity, to resist being defined by necessity. Where death is the final necessity, Christ brought resurrection. Where society was necessarily ordered and stratified along rigid ethnic lines, Christ brought reconciliation and a new order of freedom. So it is the calling of Christians to resist and refuse violence and introduce another alternative, a way of freedom.

If we join a movement, we should not participate in any of its violent acts, whether it be vandalism, arson, or murder. We should not support the violent tactics even though we support the group's claims of justice. We should bear witness to the group itself about another way and remind the group of the humanity and value of the enemy oppressor, despite how they have been treating the group. If we are part of such conflicts, Ellul urges Christians to be on the side of the poor and to look for the truly poor—the unpopular poor who have no advocates. Christians should be their advocates and use their own position to plead their case before the powerful. If they do wind up yielding to necessity and being involved in violence they should freely admit that they are doing this out of their own choice, their own fear or desperation. We must never sprinkle our wars and violence with holy water or blame what we do on God, relying on the just war tradition to explain why we acted as we did. Instead, we confess that we are sinners caught up in a sinful world.

Ellul closes by calling for what he terms "Christian radicalism" and the "violence of love." This illustrates Ellul's hard core dialectical thinking. In a world of necessity he calls for freedom. In a world of mass society he focuses on the individual. In the Here and Now God arrives as the Wholly Other. In a material world he calls for a spiritual warfare. In a world of realism he calls for radicalism. In an unloving violent era he calls for the violence of love.

Here is how he describes it: "What Christ does for us is above all to make us free . . . But to have true freedom is to escape necessity or rather to be free to struggle against necessity. Therefore I say that only one line of action is open to the Christian who is free in Christ. He must struggle against violence precisely because apart from Christ violence is the form that human relations normally and necessarily take."[3] He continues with that statement that "either we accept the order of necessity, acquiesce in and obey it . . . or else we accept the order of Christ but then we must reject violence root and branch."[4] He then adds:

3. Ellul, *Violence*, 127.
4. Ibid., 129.

And mind this means *all* kinds and ways of violence: psychological manipulation, doctrinal terrorism, economic imperialism, the venomous warfare of free competition, as well as torture, guerilla movements, police action. The capitalist who, operating from his headquarters, exploits the mass of workers or colonial peoples is just as violent as the guerilla; he must absolutely not assume the mantle of Christianity. What he does is of the order of necessity, of estrangement from God, and even if he is a faithful churchgoer and a highly educated man there is no freedom in him.[5]

Taking the above ideas into consideration, Ellul suggests that we need a renewed "Christian radicalism": "If the Christian is to contend against violence (whatever its source) he will have to be absolutely intransigent, he will have to refuse to be conciliated . . . Christian faith is radical, decisive like the very word of God, or else it is nothing."[6] This does not mean withdrawal from the world or inaction or passivity but rather full, living presence in a violent world but with something specific and unique to offer. Ellul stated that "because Christianity is the revelation of the Wholly Other, that action must be different, specific, singular, incommensurable with political or corporate methods of action."[7] It does not mean counseling the poor and oppressed to be submissive and accepting but to be their advocate, to urge their cause and call for justice.

One of Ellul's recurring themes in his other books is the importance of the "watchman on the wall" who foresees distant, approaching events and warns the city. In an era absorbed in a blizzard of "breaking news" and current events and celebrity tweets, who will play that role and foresee with greater depth and understanding coming conflicts and challenges that could well lead to violence in our streets or between nations? All too often it is when we are in the middle of a hot war or conflict that people demand insight, answers, and solutions. But by that time situations are much less fluid and amenable to change. Necessity and the laws of violence have taken over completely. So one of the ways Christians can fulfill their role in society is to try to serve as the watchman on the wall to speak and act while situations are still fluid. Where is the next Iraq or Libya or Ukraine? What can be done or said *now* to find another way than the violence that will inevitably arrive if we do nothing and allow things to develop as they are?

5. Ibid., 130–31.
6. Ibid., 145–46.
7. Ibid., 148.

Radical Christian presence should provide an inexhaustible source of creative ideas and actions for nonviolent resolution of grievances, misunderstandings, ignorance, fear, and injury. Rather than just providing analyses and justification for violent acts, followers of the Wholly Other should provide creative, constructive alternatives including diplomacy and redress of grievances. Radical Christians should be present in the movements and groups of our world but always playing the role of ambassador to the group from Christ's kingdom with its distinctive values. Helping our group to understand and see the humanity of the rival and the enemy, even becoming the enemy's advocate and protector if our side somehow wins.

In the end, what can we make of Ellul's approach to violence? In general I think that his perspectives are very insightful, important, and helpful. They certainly challenge us to think again, more deeply and carefully, about our world and its violence and coercion. All of his points are important considerations, and applying his thinking in today's world of ever-increasing violence committed on behalf of values that are claimed to be rooted in religious faith creates enormous challenges. But as I said earlier, Ellul is a prophet, not a teacher. I think the prophet is inadequate on a couple of points in particular. While I am generally in agreement about the centrality of freedom in Christian and human existence, I don't think that it can stand alone. Love and justice, for example deserve to be at the heart of our thinking as well. Necessity cannot be all bad. There is a necessity to eat, to love, to sleep, and to work. Theologically these are part of creation, not just part of the fall. That eating or working, for example, can become obsessive and toxic is part of the fallenness and brokenness of human life. So fasting and Sabbath-keeping are important acts of freedom from necessity but they don't stand alone and suggest that we stop eating or working entirely. Coercion is also part of raising children, teaching students, and managing traffic flows, but coercion needs to be evaluated and limited, and the coercers need to be held accountable. However, failing to exercise discipline or to correct the erring child, the failing student, or the speeding driver is not a choice that serves their humanity—or their freedom. So Ellul's descriptions of freedom and necessity are interesting and illuminating and challenging but insufficient.

A second problem is that by defining violence so broadly and rejecting it so completely, we are left with no criteria or method to do less damage rather than more (to say nothing of greater good, should that be possible). The just war criteria is one helpful avenue, and the chapters which follow will provide insight into Ellul's thinking on just war and violence as phenomena worthy of critical thought and analysis.

References

Baker, Mark. "Re-view: *Violence.*" *Ellul Forum* 32 (2003) 20–21.

Ellul, Jacques. *The Ethics of Freedom.* Translated by Geoffrey W. Bromiley. Grand Rapids: Eerdmans, 1976.

———. *Violence: Reflections from a Christian Perspective.* Translated by Cecilia Gaul Kings. New York: Seabury, 1969.

Gill, David W. "Violence." In *New Dictionary of Christian Ethics and Pastoral Theology,* edited by David J. Atkinson and David F. Field, 875–79. Downers Grove, IL: InterVarsity, 1995.

Goddard, Andrew. "Ellul on Violence and Just War." *Ellul Forum* 32 (2003) 3–7.

Konyndyk, Kenneth. "Violence." In *Jacques Ellul: Interpretive Essays,* edited by Clifford G. Christians and Jay M. Van Hook, 251–69. Chicago: University of Illinois Press, 1981.

Marty, Martin. "Shattered Necessities." Review of *Violence,* by Jacques Ellul. In *Christian Century* 86 (1969) 1223–24.

Yoder, John Howard. "The Casuistry of Violence." *Ellul Forum* 16 (1996) 6.

Chapter 2

Calvin, Barth, Ellul, and the Powers That Be

David Stokes

> *Let every person be subject to the governing authorities; for there is*
> *no authority except from God, and those authorities have been insti-*
> *tuted by God. Therefore whoever resists authority resists what God*
> *has appointed, and those who resist will incur judgment. For rulers*
> *are not a terror to good conduct, but to bad. Do you wish to have no*
> *fear of the authority? Then do what is good and you will receive its*
> *approval; for it is God's servant for your good. But if you do wrong,*
> *you should be afraid, for the authority does not bear the sword in*
> *vain! It is the servant of God to execute the wrongdoer. Therefore*
> *one must be subject not only because of wrath but also because of*
> *conscience. (Romans 13:1–5)[1]*

A WELL-KNOWN ANECDOTE TELLS of Karl Barth returning a photograph
of himself to an admirer. Upon it he had inscribed: To a Barthian from
one who is not a Barthian. The Swiss theologian's inscription emphasized a
point he was to make frequently throughout his five-decade dominance of
European theology. There are no set protocols by which to practice the craft
of theology. Rather, theological reflection demands that one listens to the
Word of God in obedience—without doctrinal presuppositions or systematic technique. Few admirers of Barth heeded this demand more than the
French sociologist and theologian, Jacques Ellul.

---

1. Scripture citations throughout are taken from the New Revised Standard Version.

Throughout his career, Ellul was to cite Karl Barth along with Sōren Kierkegaard as the formative touchstones in his own Christian faith. Ellul said, "Barth had an extraordinary liberating effect [on me] offering a method of comprehension far more than solutions. Calvin constantly offers answers, solutions, or a construction, while Barth launches you into an adventure."[2]

Despite the qualifications of several scholars,[3] I would argue that we are correct to call Ellul a faithful Barthian. But in doing so we need to remember that Ellul's faithfulness lies precisely in his willingness to launch out in a direction determined by a radical obedience to the Word of God, and not by dogmatic presuppositions laid down by his Swiss mentor.[4]

Nowhere do we see this creative "faithfulness" better than in Ellul's reflections on church and state. I will, therefore, concentrate here on their exegesis of Romans 13, focusing on the first four verses of this chapter. These verses, which have often been read as Paul's "theology of the state," have proven a major *crux interpretum* regarding the relationship between church and state since the seventeenth century. I begin, though, by reviewing John Calvin's exegesis of this chapter. For it is only when we set their exegesis of Romans 13 against the backdrop of the Genevan founding father's commentary, that we can comprehend the dramatic theological shift which both Barth and Ellul effected within the Reformed tradition—and, ultimately, the profound division between the two men.

In his 1539 commentary John Calvin follows the accepted division of the epistle. The first eleven chapters set out the "doctrinal" foundations of Paul's gospel—the righteousness of God, the mercy shown us in Jesus Christ, and justification by faith. The concluding four chapters present the ethical ramifications of the Christian life; focusing on how Christians ought to live in order to witness to God's righteousness.

Calvin reads chapter 12 as a charge by Paul to his fellow Christians to exercise goodwill among themselves and the larger world. For him the apostle's words are epitomized in the instruction, "Bless those who persecute you; bless and do not curse them."[5] The chapter's concluding verse directs Christians to refrain from any retaliation. "Do not be overcome

---

2. Ellul, *Perspectives on Our Age*, 14.

3. See Bromiley, "Barth's Influence on Jacques Ellul," and Clendenin, "Theological Method in Jacques Ellul."

4. See Ellul, *Ethics of Freedom*. Ellul himself can be quite critical of Barth.

5. Romans 12:14.

by evil, but overcome evil with good."[6] Calvin comments, "[If] we return good for evil, we display by that very act an invincible constancy of mind."[7]

In his exegesis of chapter 13, Calvin presents Paul as turning "outward" in order to consider Christian behavior in the public square. Significantly, he interprets verse 13:1 as arising from Paul's concern with seditious Jews who would subvert Roman authority; Calvin's fear of disorder precedes his strictures on order. Such sedition, of course, was not peculiar to the first century. Calvin noted that "there are always some restless spirits who believe that the kingdom of Christ is properly exalted only when all earthly power is abolished, and that they can enjoy the liberty which he has given them only if they have shaken off every yoke of human slavery."[8] As Calvin construes the apostle, far from understanding the eschatological imminence of God's kingdom as relativizing all earthly authority, Paul puts forward the exact opposite idea: the higher powers have been so ordered precisely to prepare for this coming kingdom.

And why does Paul refer to these earthly magistrates as "higher powers"? Calvin's answer is an example of his conviction that hierarchy has been divinely ordained not only for the church but also the state. With stunning bluntness he glosses, "By using this expression [higher powers] Paul intended, I think, to remove the empty curiosity of those who often ask by what right those who are in authority came by their power. It ought really to be sufficient for us that they rule."[9]

We should note in anticipation of our reading of Bath and especially Ellul that Calvin never identifies these "higher powers" with the "powers and principalities" of Ephesians 6:12. There is nothing whatsoever demonic or even spiritual about these powers; they are established firmly here on earth. Not that this authority is always free of fault; whatever is, is not necessarily right. Magistrates may, indeed do, prove to be abusive. Nevertheless, Christians are not to depart from the obedience owed them, since magistrates, even in spite of themselves, rule for the common good.[10] Calvin is quick, though, to explain what lies behind civil misrule. "If a wicked ruler is the Lord's scourge to punish the sins of the people, let us reflect that it is

---

6. Romans 12:21.

7. Calvin, *Epistles of Paul the Apostle*, 279.

8. Ibid., 280.

9. Ibid.

10. Ibid., 282.

our own fault that this excellent blessing of God is turned into a curse."[11] Christians deserve what they receive. Indeed, Calvin comments on one of the classic paradoxes of the Reformation, "No tyranny . . . can exist which does not in some respect assist in protecting human society."[12]

He is brief in describing the positive duties of these magistrates; he seems to take for granted the purpose of government. "He [God] has appointed [magistrates] for the just and lawful government of the world."[13] Simply put, magistrates possess an obvious utility. And, to this end, they wield a two-edged sword: "to provide for the peace of the good, and to restrain the waywardness of the wicked."[14] Calvin here presents government as a limited concept; its purpose is to protect ourselves from ourselves, no less, but certainly no more.

Paul finally arrives at his principle point. What role ought the Christian to play in this hierarchy? We are to be obedient *tout court*. The Christian is charged to obedience "not only on the ground of human necessity, but also in order to obey God."[15] To obey is to come to know. And the magistrates are the very agents by which we come to know the will of God. Therefore "[t]he individual does not have the right to deprive of his authority the one who is set in power over us by the Lord."[16] Calvin concludes his reading, though, with words that demand our attention. He wrote, "the whole of this discussion concerns civil government. Those, therefore, who bear rule over men's consciences attempt to establish their blasphemous tyranny in vain."[17] What Calvin exegetically grants with one hand, he subverts with the other: the tyrant may assist in protecting human society and still be a tyrant; he may govern for the sake of the public good, all-the-while being of the devil's party.

In the twenty years between his Romans commentary and the subsequent editions of his *Institutes*, Calvin expanded his comments on the function of government and modified his views on tyrannous magistrates. These two decades of Genevan rule seems to have woven into Calvin's conservatism a certain implicit radicalism. Significantly, Calvin places

11. Ibid.

12. Ibid., 282.

13. Ibid., 281.

14. Ibid.

15. Ibid.

16. Ibid., 283.

17. Ibid.

these comments at the end of Book IV, "The External Means or Aims by Which God Invites Us Into the Society of Christ and Holds Us Therein." On the one hand, he reaffirms his belief that government need not be a "thing polluted." Just as Paul admonishes subversive Jews who question Roman authority, Calvin criticizes those radical Reformers who judge earthly laws as beneath the Christian. Indeed, the spiritual government of the city has already initiated "in us upon earth certain beginnings of the Heavenly Kingdom, and in this mortal and fleeting life affords us a certain forecast of an immortal and incorruptible blessedness."[18] In the *Institutes,* Calvin has greatly expanded on the ends ordained for government; the magistrates are charged with nothing less than "to cherish and protect the outward worship of God, to defend sound doctrine of piety and the position of the church, to adjust our life to the society of men, to form our social behavior to civil righteousness, to reconcile us with one another, and to promote general peace and tranquility."[19] Whereas Calvin considers the functions of church and state separately in his Romans commentary, he presents them as complementary in his *Institutes.*

On the other hand, whatever obedience we owe our rulers, however much the wicked ruler may be a judgment of God, Calvin concludes, "In that obedience which we have shown to be due the authority of rulers, we are always to make this exception, indeed, to observe it as primary, that such obedience is never to lead us away from obedience to him [God], to whose will the desires of all kings ought to be subject, to whose decrees all their commands ought to yield, to whose majesty their scepters ought to be submitted."[20] Magistrates such as kings have limits which they must not exceed. Calvin then states, in order for us to keep our courage, "Paul pricks us with another goad: That we have been redeemed by Christ at so great a price as our redemption cost him, so that we should not enslave ourselves to the wicked desires of men—much less be subject to their impiety."[21] Calvin's cautionary conclusion remains quite general; the precise nature of these limits goes unstated. Yet these final few sentences have left theologians over the last four hundred years—especially Barth and Ellul—with a challenge and a problem: the nature of Christian freedom before the powers-that-be. When we move from Calvin's 1539 commentary on Romans to Karl Barth's

18. Calvin, *Institutes of the Christian Religion,* 1487.

19. Ibid.

20. Ibid., 1520.

21. Ibid., 1521.

1921 *Römerbrief*, we move from a theologian who finds in Romans 13 a divine mandate for civic order, to a theologian who finds an eschatological challenge to all human order.

Unlike Calvin, Barth reads Romans 13:1–2 as a development of the preceding verse [12:21], *Be not overcome of evil, but overcome evil with good.* The apostle is not moving from Christian communal ethics "outward" to ethics of the public square. Instead, he is simply elaborating on the truth—"The Great Disturbance"—revealed by the "Moment" of Jesus Christ. This Moment has forever qualified "the temporal past and the temporal future."[22] Paul charges Christians to overcome evil with good because in the light of the Moment "the more successfully the good and the right assume concrete form, the more they become evil . . . ."[23] Christians are to oppose good with evil not because it is a virtuous thing to do, but by doing so, by their engagement in such "negative" behavior, Christians expose the existing powers—the status quo—for what they are. Every man is subject to the existing ruling powers, but he is subject as a *negative* witness against those powers. To rebel against these powers is to give their influence over our lives an even greater pathos. Instead, "no-revolution is the best preparation for the true Revolution . . . ."[24] This is decidedly not Calvin's world of duly ordained magistrates and dutiful citizens.

Barth lists these powers in a series of upper-case nouns: State, Church, Society, Positive Right, and Organized Research; this subset possesses all the menace of Milton's catalogue of demons. It would be incorrect to say that Barth spiritualizes the powers-that-be. But his rhetoric, typical of the *Römerbrief*, renders these powers almost as cosmic hypostases. Thus, "[a]ll human consciousness, all human principles and axioms and orthodoxies and –isms, all *principalities and power and dominion,* are *as such* subjected to the destructive judgment of God."[25] As we will see, informed by his understanding of the pervasiveness of technological society, Ellul will take much more seriously than Barth the reality of such an hypostatization.

Barth's dialectics force him to go further, though. The Christian non-revolutionary is forever tempted to imagine that his or her exposure of the existing order is a prelude to the inauguration of a proper order. The Christian is tempted to understand this *of God* as a mirroring of human

22. Barth, *Epistle to the Romans*, 476.
23. Ibid., 479.
24. Ibid., 483.
25. Ibid. Emphasis in the original.

aspirations. The revolutionaries of today become tomorrow's oppressive powers. Barth refers to such "Legitimism" as possessing an inherent arrogant and titanic element the equal of any existing power it opposes. Barth counters, "He of whom the *power* is and by whom every existing authority is ordained is God the Lord, the Unknown, Hidden God, Creator and Redeemer, the God who elects and rejects."[26] Vengeance belongs to God, never to the Christian. "Even the observer who has been directly hurt and wounded by the evil of the existing order must bow before Him who is so strong and wondrous a God, high above all gods."[27]

The powers-that-be, positive as well as negative, remain—must remain—an eschatological sign for the One who is to come. Barth writes in imagery far removed from Calvin's world, "Where is there . . . evil which is not pregnant with witness to the good? Where is there any concrete thing which is not pregnant with that which is Primal and invisible? Is not, therefore, the existing order a pregnant parable of the Order that does not exist?"[28]

In the *Römerbrief II* we do not find any suggestion that the Christian, or the church itself, might be called upon to oppose, much less question, the present order of things. Barth's comments on the Christian's role in society are elliptical, more suggestive than substantive. Instead of showing the church as complementary to the state, Barth suggests that the church's proper witness is one of sectarian passivity. Regarding Paul's command that we are to be *subject* to the existing powers, "Our subjection means . . . no more than that vengeance is not our affair. It means that the divine minus before the bracket (around the existing powers) must not be deprived of its potency by a series of anticipatory negations on our part."[29] Throughout this section of the *Römerbrief* Barth says little about the corporate nature of the church. Instead, he reads Romans 13 as addressed primarily to the individual Christian.

And yet, much like the Calvin of the *Institutes*, in the twenty years which separate his *Römerbrief* and the *Church Dogmatics: The Doctrine of God II.2*, cataclysmic historic events force Barth to return to Romans 13 in an extended excursus in the chapter, "The Command of God as the Decision of God." The Calvin of the *Institutes* appends his strictures on the

26. Ibid., 484.
27. Ibid.
28. Ibid., 485.
29. Ibid.,

state and church to his *ordering* of the church, the Barth of the *Dogmatics* incorporates his remarks on church and state *within* his development of the ethics determined by the graciousness of God as revealed in Jesus Christ. A much expanded Christology has come to replace the actualistic nature of the "Moment" which we find in the *Römerbrief*.

Whereas the eschatological "Moment" calls into question all human endeavors, the command of God, as effected by Jesus Christ, addresses all people. Instead of being concerned only with the Christian community, Romans 12 "contains directions about the life of Christians in relationship with others: first . . . their fellowship among themselves, and then . . . their contacts with the surrounding non-Christian world."[30] Barth's tone does not set Christians against the world, but puts Christians in solidarity with the world. Consequently, he comments upon Paul's charge in Romans 13:8 to owe no one anything except to love one another: "What Christians decidedly owe to the world . . . is just that they should love one another in this way. In so far as this love is alive among Christians . . . the Church is edified, the good work which God requires takes place, not only in the inner circle of Christians, but with the creation and maintenance of this circle for everyone and the whole world."[31]

Barth repeats the warning of what he has written twenty years earlier: Christians "do not fight in their own cause, and they cannot, therefore, wish to vindicate their right when a wrong is done them."[32] God will accomplish his purposes in the ways he chooses. And yet the divine command places before Christians a certain responsibility; he or she is not consigned to a sectarian passivity. Barth wrote, "even as Christians they are responsible, according to [Romans] 13:1, for seeing that it [God's will] is done at the right time and in the way God has ordained. Because they do not evade this responsibility, because they give the wrath of God its due place, they go beyond this place, for they do not know about the wrath of God, but realize His wrath is the burning of His love."[33] God's command has so positioned the Church that it understands Caesar better than Caesar understands himself.

True, Barth is able to sound very much like his younger self in this excursus. The dialectic of the *Römerbrief* remains. Both church and state

---

30. Barth, *Church Dogmatics*, 719.

31. Ibid.

32. Ibid., 720.

33. Ibid.

rest on the same provisional foundations; the "form of this world," although defeated by Jesus Christ, still exercises a qualified power over both even in its defeat. And yet, as Barth now read Romans, the non-Christian world—Caesar—no longer lies outside the kingdom of Christ; the state is no longer simply an enigmatic parable of what is to be. Both church and state "are servants, each serving the Lord with their better or less good faith, each finding in the Lord his own Judge and Saviour. They cannot exclude each other when God has accepted both and will judge their faithfulness or unfaithfulness by His mercy."[34]

Barth concludes, "No objective right ever permits any of us [within the church] not to walk in love, to bring to ruin those for whom Christ died. In common with them . . . and therefore in a concern for our own faith, we must secure the good of God's kingdom and not the good of our own better faith and better way. Let us show the superior soundness of our own faith by unhesitatingly preferring to our own objective right our concern for the peace and common edification of the Church and therefore for the faith of our neighbor."[35]

Like Calvin and Barth, Jacques Ellul offered an exegesis of Romans 13. Unlike Calvin and Barth he does not consider this chapter within commentary on the epistle. Rather it is found in a brief but trenchant study on Christianity and anarchy, published after Ellul's death. The specific exegesis appears in the chapter "The Bible as a Source of Anarchy." Far from its location being an incidental detail, context here is everything. It prepares us for Ellul's reading of Paul—indeed of the entire Bible—which is decidedly cross-grained to the Reformed tradition—and to Barth. We cannot discuss his interpretation of Romans 13 abstracted from his survey of those biblical texts which precede it—what Ellul calls his "naïve" reading of Scripture.

He begins his consideration of "The Bible as a Source of Anarchy" with a review of Hebrew scripture. Whereas many scholars might begin with the Exodus or Patriarchal tradition, Ellul begins with the histories of Israel's judges and kings. Ellul accentuates the ambiguity towards the Davidic throne throughout the books of Samuel and Kings. The "good" kings are defeated in battle, whereas the "great" kings, who do achieve military success, reject God and promote idolatry. He proceeds to summarize the prophetic books in so far as they reinforce this same anti-monarchist theme. Prophet after prophet stands as a counterbalance to tyrannical

34. Ibid., 725.
35. Ibid., 725–26.

kings, a "true" prophet defeats a "false" prophet."[36] And then turning to the Wisdom literature of the fourth century BCE, Ellul finds a "virulent attack on all domination. God's response to Israel's prayer that they be given a king like all the other nations yields bitter fruit, and can be seen in such statements as 'do not curse the king, even in your thoughts, or curse the rich even in your bedroom; for a bird of the air may carry your voice, or some winged creature tell the matter.'"[37]

Next, whereas a majority of New Testament scholars usually bridge Old and New Testaments by considering the Pauline epistles, Ellul gives us an overview of the gospels' accounts which concern authority and power. The coin owed Caesar, Jesus' discussion with his disciples regarding the nature of discipleship, the swords Peter is ordered to sheath—the three incidents share a common theme: the light of Christ reveals all earthly politics either as derivative of divine authority or, as is more likely, grounded in demonic power.

Ellul's unique reading of John 19:11 (foundational for Barth in establishing that political power is from God) takes the verse to epitomize the gospels' judgement of all human authority. In response to Pilate's question whether he knows that Pilate has the power to release him, Jesus answers, "You would have no power over me unless it had been given you from above; therefore the one who handed me over to you is guilty of a greater sin." Ellul argues that given the second part of this reply, "from above," is synonymous with "from an evil spirit." Just as the Satan of the Temptation stories has power over the nations of the world, so he has power to establish Pilate. If Caesar is behind the Roman governor, the demonic is behind Caesar.

Ellul then turns to the two beasts of chapter 13 of the Apocalypse— the book of Revelation, the entire book of which "is a challenge to political power."[38] Ellul follows the traditional reading that the beast (from the sea) is Rome. But his reading of the second beast (from the earth) departs radically from the standard commentaries, which hold that "It exercises all the authority of the first beast on its behalf, and it makes the earth and its inhabitants worship the first beast."[39] Instead of taking this second beast to be some unnamed false prophet, Ellul argues that it is an elaborate allegory

36. Ellul, *Anarchy and Christianity*, 52.
37. Ecclesiastes 10:20.
38. Ellul, *Anarchy and Christianity*, 72.
39. Revelation 13:12.

of the military agents of Roman propaganda, that is, those who would enforce the cult of the Roman emperor. What Revelation is condemning is not simply Roman imperialism and its incursion into Israel, but the totalitarianism which comes with the spread of empire.

On this note, Ellul finally turns to Paul. He reads Romans 13:1–5 as the only ones in the Bible that stress obedience to authority. Most commentators (such as Calvin, but not the Barth of the *Römerbrief*) have placed the accent on verse 1, that all authority comes from God. In doing so, they overlook the sequence of Paul's argument, founded upon "Bless those who persecute you; bless and do not curse."[40] Paul's command applies first to fellow Christians, then to their fellow human beings, and *now* (in chapter 13) to those *individuals* who comprise the government. His charge is much the same as Jesus' instructions to render unto Caesar what belongs to Caesar, which, in keeping with Ellul's larger reading of the New Testament, means that we owe neither respect nor honor to magistrates and authorities—"the only one to whom honor is due is God."[41] There are only two things the Christian owes the powers-that-be. First, fulfillment of their "civic duties", e.g., the paying of taxes. Second, and much more importantly for Ellul's project, prayer on their behalf—prayer for their conversion, and not that they may stay in power!

Ellul concludes his consideration of Paul with Lutheran theologian Oscar Cullmann's argument of some forty years earlier, that Paul also uses the word for authority (*exousiai*) to refer to abstract religious powers, celestial as well as demonic. "He [Jesus] disarmed the rulers and authorities and made a public example of them, triumphing over them in it [the cross]."[42] When we take into account this meaning of authority, "the New Testament leads us to suppose that earthly political and military authorities really have their basis in an alliance with spiritual powers, which I will not call celestial, since they might equally well be evil and demonic. The existence of these spiritual *exousiai* would explain the universality of political powers and also the astonishing fact that people obey them as though it were self-evident."[43] In aligning himself with Cullmann, Ellul recalls the Barth of the *Römerbrief.* And yet what for the early Barth is a parabolic way of speaking is for Ellul the very essence of the New Testament's witness

---

40. Romans 12:14.

41. Ellul, *Anarchy and Christianity*, 81.

42. Colossians 2:15.

43. Ellul, *Anarchy and Christianity*, 83.

regarding earthly authority. The powers-that-be, far from being harbingers for the coming kingdom, have been rendered by Jesus powers which have no ultimate power.

John Calvin laid the foundation of what we may call the mainline Reformed view that the City of Man and the City of God, both divinely ordained, have complementary purposes; the former overseeing humanity's civic welfare, the latter humanity's spiritual welfare. The word *complementary* here is critical in understanding how church and state ought to relate one to another. The state was not to be thought of as founded on the church, a theocracy as imagined by many medieval canonists. Nor was it an earthly administrator of God's will radically juxtaposed to the kingdom of God, as Luther depicted it. Rather church and state, when rightly ordered, possess a symbiotic relationship by which men and women, body and soul, are nurtured. And yet, in so far that Calvin blended both medieval and Lutheran thought, the state had specific limits it could not trespass without being judged by the church.

The Barth of the *Römerbrief* retains much of Calvin's vocabulary, but, as we have seen, transposes it to a very different key. The powers-that-be are indeed ordained by God but ordained to be a confounding parable; it exposes not only our human limitation but our monstrous pride. And so it provokes the Christian to what we might call an eschatological passivity; Christians are to be obedient in order to prove themselves a sign of contradiction to all that the state is and is *not*. But the Barth of the *Dogmatics* changes course, all-the-while retaining his former vocabulary. The powers-that-be are indeed parabolic of the coming kingdom, and yet, for the later Barth, parabolic in a *positive* sense; the state is capable of witnessing, however indirectly, to what has been established, already and yet to come, in Jesus Christ. Consequently, the church's role—the obedience to which Paul calls it—consists in recalling the state to what God has willed it to be, that is, a herald of God's coming kingdom. The church does not stand in judgment of the state, but finds itself tasked to proclaim repeatedly: Become what you are.

Ellul agrees with Barth's foundational presuppositions. The inclusive finality of the work of Christ, the church's role in proclaiming this finality, and Christian faith as a concern for the edification of our neighbor and the great commonwealth. Where Ellul departs dramatically from Barth is in his understanding of the state. The state remains for Barth—both the Barth of the *Römerbrief* and of the *Dogmatics*—what it has been for the Protestant theologians who preceded him: a clearly defined body by which civic welfare is regulated. For Ellul the (modern) state has become what Revelation (and Paul) anticipated:

> The result is that political power is not a final court. It is always relative. We can expect from it only what is relative and open to question. This is the meaning of Paul's statement and it shows how much we need to relativize the (traditionally absolutized) formula that there is no authority except from God. Power is indeed from God, but all power is overcome in Christ![44]

The differences between the ethical ramifications that result from Ellul's and Barth's rendering of Romans 13 are considerable, especially as they relate to war and violence. And it would take a lengthier essay to explore them in depth. But for now, by way of conclusion, let me offer a precis of such an essay.

Confronted by the Word of God, the Barth of post-First World War Europe—the "early" Barth of the *Römerbrief*—understood the powers-that-be as one of several dark parables where time and eternity intersect, while the "later" Barth of the Second World War—the Barth of the *Dogmatics*—understood these powers to be potential servants of the same Lord whom the church served. Confronted by the same Word of God, the Jacques Ellul of a postwar world understood the powers-that-be to be a vast technological net in which all humanity is entangled, its power rendered powerless by the power of Jesus Christ. Both men in their times were obedient to the freedom of the Word of God. And by his obedience Ellul showed himself to be a faithful Barthian—even when the obedience placed him at odds with Barth!

References

Barth, Karl. *Church Dogmatics: Doctrine of God* II. 2. Translated by Geoffrey W. Bromiley et al. Edinburgh: T. & T. Clark, 1957.
———. *The Epistle to the Romans*. Translated by Edwyn C. Hoskyns. London: Oxford University Press, 1933.
Bromiley, Geoffrey. "Barth's Influence on Jacques Ellul." In *Jacques Ellul: Interpretive Essays,* edited by Clifford G. Christians and Jay M. Hook, 32–52. Chicago: University of Illinois Press, 1981.
Calvin, John. *Epistles of Paul the Apostle to the Romans and to the Thessalonians.* Translated by Ross Mackenzie. Edinburgh: Saint Andrew, 1961.

44. Ellul, *Anarchy and Christianity*, 84–85.

————. *Institutes of the Christian Religion*, vol. II. The Library of Christian Classics. Translated by Ford Lewis Battles. Philadelphia: Westminster, 1960.

Clendenin, Daniel B. *Theological Method in Jacques Ellul*. Lanham MD: University Press of America, 1987.

Ellul, Jacques. *Anarchy and Christianity*. Translated by Geoffrey W. Bromiley. Eugene, OR: Wipf & Stock, 2011.

————. *The Ethics of Freedom*. London: Mowbrays, 1976.

————. *Perspectives on Our Age: Jacques Ellul Speaks on His Life and Work*. Edited by Willem H. Vanderburg, Toronto: House of Anansi, 2004.

Chapter 3

Ellul on Violence and Just War[1]

Andrew Goddard

THE QUESTION OF WHAT faithful disciples of Jesus are to say and to do in response to the violence of war has divided Christians for most of the history of the church. As Ellul states in the opening sentence of his book on the subject of violence, "The churches and theologians . . . have never been in unanimous agreement in their views on violence in human society."[2] That does not, however, mean that there has not been a consensus down the centuries. There has clearly been a predominant approach to the question of war, namely that of the "just war tradition" which has argued that political authority can, subject to various constraints, legitimately use lethal military force outside its sphere of jurisdiction in the pursuit of justice.[3] With pre-Christian origins, it took a distinctively Christian form in the writings of Augustine which in turn shaped both medieval theologians such as Aquinas and the Reformers.[4]

Ellul is a trenchant critic of this way of thinking and yet, as often is this case in his writing, his comments are lacking in detailed engagement

1. This chapter is a revised version of an article that first appeared in the *Ellul Forum* 32 (2003).

2. Ellul, *Violence*, 1. There are discussions of war in other works by Ellul and in various articles, including a number now collected in Ellul, *Israel: Chance de Civilisation*, 254–56, where we see especially "*Guerre juste . . . Ce que j'en pense.*"

3. One of the best recent articulations of this tradition is Biggar, *In Defence of War*.

4. An excellent reader with major texts is Reichberg, *The Ethics of War* and Reichberg *Religion, War and Ethics* which draws from writings from a range of religious traditions including Christianity.

with the specific arguments of his opponents. Instead, he provides a broad-brush account and critique. This, while making some strong and valid objections, is bound to leave anyone sympathetic to the complexities of the just war tradition feeling rather dissatisfied, perhaps even that they have been subjected to the "violence" of caricature.[5]

Given the importance of this subject and the strong differences of opinion found among Christians resulting in divided witness to the world, it is necessary to step back and identify the fundamental differences between the just war tradition and Ellul's thinking and to ascertain whether any constructive dialogue can take place between them. This chapter highlights two areas in which the wider rationale and method of Ellul and the just war tradition stand in tension with each other and acknowledges both strengths and weaknesses that can be seen when the two approaches are placed in dialogue.

The heart of the divergence between Ellul's account of violence and that of the mainstream Christian tradition is perhaps most easily understood by reference to the two terms which identify that tradition—"just war." In relation to these two terms, Ellul questions both the proper focus and subject matter (writing on violence rather than war) and the moral purpose and task (which he argues should be confession of sin and not justification).

The Subject Matter—War or Violence?

It is of the utmost importance that Ellul's account is focussed on *violence*, and interestingly, in the original French is entitled *Contre les violents*.[6] The specific question of *war* is therefore set in the wider context of the phenom-

5. The main critiques and account of the historical origins of the tradition are found in his categorization of this approach as one of "compromise." See Ellul, *Violence*, 1–9, and his appendix on conscientious objection in Ellul, *Anarchy and Christianity*, 91–95. A less polemical account of the origins of the Christian just war tradition is found in his study of the history of institutions in Ellul, *Histoire des Institutions Vol 2*, 506–7, 525–27. Particularly given our current context, it is also important to note that he sees this tradition in part shaped by Islam's subversion of Christian faith, see Ellul, *Subversion of Christianity*, 100–104. This chapter from *Subversion* is reprinted and the theme of Islam and war also explored in other chapters in Ellul, *Islam and Judaeo-Christianity*.

6. Ellul's main concern appears to be, as often in his work (for example in *False Presence of the Kingdom* and *Jesus and Marx*), those Christians who are similar to him in their advocacy of a radical, revolutionary Christian faith but who have from his perspective taken a serious false step by supporting and justifying violence in their cause.

enon of *violence*. Instead of concentrating on the definition of war that one would find in the Oxford English Dictionary, which is "hostile contention by means of armed forces, carried on between nations, states, or rulers, or between parties in the same nation or state; the employment of armed forces against a foreign power, or against an opposing party in the state," he insists that thinking about this specific subject can only be properly done once set in a wider context. To think rightly about war there is the need, in the words of the title of his book's third chapter, for "Christian realism in the face of violence."

This approach marks a significant shift in understanding of the question. The great Christian theologians of the just war tradition generally approach their discussion from two angles. In some contexts, it is a question about how a confessing Christian with a particular political or military responsibility in society is to act or indeed whether they can faithfully remain in certain positions given the duties that will be incumbent upon them.[7] In others, it is seeking to elucidate the obligations of love and the prohibitions entailed by the specific commandment against murder.[8] In thinking about "war," in other words, we are being asked to reflect on a form of practical, political action that raises a fundamental moral question because it requires participants to be involved in the taking of human life.

Ellul, from the opening pages of his book, critiques this tradition by relocating it within his own predominant category of violence. So, categorizing this strand of Christian thinking as "compromise," he places the early Christian concerns about the state in relation to "violence"—"they saw that the state . . . used violence against its enemies, internal or external. For war certainly seemed violence pure and simple, and the police operated by violence."[9] The challenge that remained even when Christians held political office and the state ceased persecution of the church is expressed in the following terms—"the political power . . . continued to use violence."[10] Ellul

---

7. Among the key classic texts in the just war tradition are Augustine's letter to Count Boniface (Letter 189, from 418 CE) with the counsel, "Do not think that it is impossible for any one to please God while engaged in active military service" and Martin Luther's "Whether Soldiers, too, Can be Saved" (1526), written to respond to the concerns of Assa von Kram of Wittenberg about reconciling his Christian faith and military profession.

8. Thus Thomas Aquinas' main discussions in the *Summa* are (a) *ST* II-II, q40 which is entitled "Of War" and, importantly, placed under the discussion of charity, and (b) *ST II-II*, q64 "Of Murder."

9. Ellul, *Violence*, 2.

10. Ibid., 3.

then explains how theologians and canonists responded to this challenge which he insists on describing as "internal violence" and "external violence" by the state.

In relation to internal violence, Ellul discerns two key redefinitions taking place. A distinction is drawn between the state and human beings and it is held that the state "never acts by violence when it constrains, condemns and kills."[11] Instead, its actions are distinguished from "violence" by being conceived of as "force" so that the state "is the institution which demonstrates the difference between violence and force . . . . There is all the difference between violence and force."[12] The issue then becomes whether or not the state's use of force is "just" or "unjust" and in deciding this it is conformity to the laws which is the determinative factor. However, even when the state does not conform to the laws it still uses force—albeit now unjust force—rather than violence. This reasoning, Ellul claims, was an attempt "to clear the state of the charge of violence by explaining that it was not violence."[13]

In relation to the external violence of war, Ellul believes that the church reasoned that because "to deny the state the right to go to war was to condemn it to extinction" yet the state was ordained by God, therefore the state "must have the right to wage war."[14] This he claims (though without citing any supporting evidence[15]) was the origin and fundamental rationale for "the casuistry of the just war" whose evolving tradition he sums up in

11. Ibid., 4.

12. Ibid.

13. Ibid., 5. In our current context such an analysis raises interesting questions for those who accept this distinction: Al-Qaeda was clearly a non-state body which did not present itself as taking on the responsibilities of political authority more broadly and so would be classed as using violence. We now face the new challenge of Islamic State, a group which in many ways appears more violent in its actions of beheadings, etc., but on this analysis could be described as using force as it has proclaimed a Caliphate, governs a significant amount of territory, and seeks to order social life in that sphere, not simply to attack those it perceives as enemies.

14. Ibid.

15. O'Donovan, *The Just War Revisited*, 9. O'Donovan is clear, and presents a better historical and theological account, when he writes that the Christian just war tradition is "irreconcilable" with those who "make *survival* the final criterion of what may and may not be done." He is clear, in defending just war, that "to take survival as the bottom line is to revert to the antagonistic model of mortal combat, and so inevitably to retreat from the Gospel proclamation of the universal rule of Christ and from the praxis of loving judgment. When self-defense, of state, community or individual, has the last word, paganism is restored."

terms of seven conditions to make a war just. Although Ellul acknowledges these conditions "have theoretical solidity" he questions their practicality and relevance, especially in the contemporary world.[16]

Ellul's own contrasting approach to the question is shaped by what he calls "Christian realism"—"the Christian who wants to find out what he ought to do, must be realistic; this is the first step."[17] The problem is that we need first to be clear what the Christian must be realistic about and herein lies the fundamental weakness of Ellul's work. Violence is the lens through which he reinterprets and critiques the just war tradition and the phenomenon about which he insists we must be realistic. But Ellul never clearly defines violence.[18] Certainly it is broader than the just war tradition's focus on the taking of human life but just how broad it is remains unclear. The signs are, however, that for Ellul the term is exceedingly wide-ranging in its scope—"economic relations, class relations, are relations of violence, nothing else."[19] He continues with "psychological violence . . . is simply violence, whether it takes the form of propaganda, biased reports, meetings of secret societies that inflate the egos of their members, brainwashing or intellectual terrorism."[20] It would appear that Konyndyk is broadly correct that violent behaviour for Ellul is "coercing someone in a way that violates his personhood," a very broad definition which in turn requires more clarity as to what violates personhood.[21] Given that violence is to be the overarching interpretative category for Christian reflection on war and is being used to explain Christian moral assessments in history which did not themselves primarily use this category, it would help if such a definition—or preferably a more precise one—had been given and defended by Ellul himself.

Despite this weakness, there are two great strengths in Ellul's approach. Firstly, it refuses to mask the fact that punitive measures taken by political authority have the same basic structure as the wrong actions to which they respond. So fines (like stealing) take away people's property without their consent, imprisonment (like kidnapping) deprives a person of their liberty.

16. Ellul, *Violence*, 6.

17. Ibid., 83.

18. This is a common criticism of Ellul's writing on this subject. For example, "The first question, then would seem to be: What is violence? But, strangely, Ellul does not address it." See Konyndyk, "Violence," 256. For a similar critique, extended by Ellul's positive talk of "spiritual violence," see Rognon, *Une Pensee en Dialogue*, 145 note 15.

19. Ellul, *Violence*, 86.

20. Ibid., 97.

21. Konyndyk, "Violence," 256.

Although this should be more obvious in war, the language of "force" means that it can be effectively forgotten. As Jonathan Glover comments, "It is widely held that killing in war is quite different. It is not, and we need to think about the implications of this."[22] But this similarity need not mean moral identity or that ethical differentiation is impossible or illegitimate: materially the act of sexual intercourse has a common structure whether it is joyful marital sex, adultery, fornication, or rape; the insertion of a knife into human flesh could be an act of surgery or grievous bodily harm. Ellul formulates a stark law of the identity or sameness of all violence. This, when it is given a moral focus in order to insist that we cannot distinguish between just and unjust violence or violence that liberates and violence that enslaves, simply asserts what really needs to be argued for.[23]

Secondly, Ellul also helpfully highlights the continuity between the internal coercive actions of political authority ("police functions" as we might call them) and the external actions (military functions in war). Here there is continuity between Ellul and the traditional just war understanding. That tradition similarly refuses to treat these as two independent spheres with different moralities or criteria for action. Ellul thus will be sympathetic to a common critique made by just war theorists. They point out that there is a tension (if not incoherence) in being a principled advocate of non-violent pacifism who rejects all war but not being a non-violent anarchist (Ellul is here coherent given his defense of non-violent anarchism). Similarly there are ethical challenges which are not always recognized in being committed to just war thinking but absolutely opposed in all circumstances to capital punishment (which is increasingly becoming the dominant Christian position).

Where Ellul differs fundamentally with the just war tradition is that it is marked by seeing the task of political authority as one which can legitimately be fulfilled—at home and abroad, through police and through military—through the subordination of all uses of "violence" to the pursuit of justice and the task of good judgment. Ellul himself held such views earlier in his life as is evident from his first published book on the theological foundation of law which appeared in French shortly after the war in 1946.

22. Glover, *Causing Death and Saving Lives*, 251. For a vivid, first-hand reflection on the realities of war see Marlantes, *What It Is Like To Go To War*.

23. For a more sustained philosophical argument for the moral identity of killing in war with other forms of killing, which thereby critiques just war thinking while also disagreeing with Ellul in that it seeks to justify some forms of killing, see McMahan, *Killing in War*.

There, in discussing biblical texts such as Romans 13 on the "use of the sword," he writes,

> The use of the sword in itself is not condemned . . . The use is subject to eventual condemnation . . . which will become a reality only if the sword . . . serves either the obstruction of justice or the spirit of power. Within this eschatological perspective, man's judgment in the realm of law assumes its rightful value. His judgment is the reason why the use of the sword will not be condemned. Any use of it apart from man's judgment runs counter to God's will . . . . It is law which, before God, permits the use of force.[24]

Although it is difficult to be clear as to why Ellul departed from this viewpoint, one factor is perhaps found in his comment that the just war tradition is "based on the conviction that man can retain control of violence, that violence can be kept in the service of order and justice and even of peace."[25] Ellul's later realism about violence appears to have led him to reject this fundamental presupposition which is essential to just war thinking. That realism is an important challenge to those who believe that the forms of violence found in warfare can be a valid means of enacting judgment and serving peace. Nevertheless, it is hard to dismiss the view that, at least in some cases, a limited amount of authorized force can indeed serve order, justice, and peace. If "peacekeepers" had used such controlled and limited "violence" at the start of the Rwandan genocide or in Srebrenica during the Bosnian conflict, then great evils may well have been prevented. Here, and elsewhere, order, justice, and peace may well have been served by what Ellul rejects as "violence" in a way that they were not by the refusal of UN peacekeepers to resist and suppress those bent on mass killing.[26]

In contrast to the just war tradition and his own early views, not only does Ellul place all reflection about war under the broader rubric and laws of violence, he also sees violence (and so war as a subset within that) as a force which rules human beings. Occasionally in his writing he relates this to his theological understanding of the principalities and powers by naming violence as "one of the 'rudiments' (*stoicheia*) of this world."[27] This is a

---

24. Ellul, *The Theological Foundation of Law*, 113.

25. Ellul, *Violence*, 5–6.

26. See the powerful accounts in Neuffer, *The Key To My Neighbor's House*, where chapter 5 describes the failure of UN forces in Rwanda and chapter 6 in Srebrenica.

27. Ellul, *Prayer and Modern Man*, 174. The best account on Ellul and the powers remains the work of Marva Dawn whose findings in her doctoral thesis are most easily

feature of Ellul's work on violence which frustratingly he does not develop. Its reminder of the need to consider the powers in any thinking about war stands, however, as a further challenge to the just war tradition. In making judgments about war, and assessing moral questions in relation to any particular war, we must keep sight of the bigger picture and avoid thinking ethics can simply focus on the choices and actions of individual agents abstracted and isolated from the reality of power in wider society.[28] Ellul, by approaching the question through the category of "violence" as a power in human culture, helpfully draws attention to the flaws and dangers in making moral judgments about particular actions before and during war—the classic questions relating to *jus ad bellum* and *jus in bello*—without our moral thinking and evaluation also considering the spiritual reality of the powers in the wider shaping of our society.

The Purpose—Justification or Confession?

Ellul's differences with the just war tradition are not limited to his insistence on approaching the subject of war through the much larger category of violence which is then understood in a much more global and quasi-deterministic fashion. He also has a fundamental objection to its attempt to provide justification for certain violent actions. This objection would appear to take two forms.

First, in his realistic analysis of violence, one of the features Ellul identifies—his fifth and final law of violence—is that "the man who uses violence always tries to justify both it and himself."[29] The horror and agony caused by violence means, he claims, that everyone who uses it seeks to demonstrate that they have acted morally when they have turned to violence. More controversial still Ellul explains that this universality of justification derives from the fact that "violence is an expression of hatred, has its source in hatred and signifies hatred . . . It is absolutely essential for us to realize that there is an unbreakable link between violence and hatred."[30]

---

found in "The Biblical Concept of 'the Principalities and Powers': John Yoder Points to Jacques Ellul," in Hauerwas, *The Wisdom of the Cross: Essays in Honor of John Howard Yoder*, 168–86.

28. For a recent analysis of modern warfare which helps us set ethical questions about war in this wider context, particularly of the arms industry, see Storkey, *War or Peace?*

29. Ellul, *Violence*, 103.

30. Ibid., 104.

Again this is not defended but simply repudiates the Augustinian strand of the just war tradition which appeals to "love of neighbor"—the neighbor suffering unjust oppression or violence—as its rationale for the use of coercive force. The just war tradition is, therefore, in Ellul's eyes simply one of the multiple forms of self-justification inevitably developed by fallen human beings in the face of their own violence.

Second, although Ellul can apparently accept that Christians will use violence, he refuses to accept their justifications for this. Instead, he emphasises that "as Christians we must firmly refuse to accept whatever justifications are advanced."[31] He is insistent that "in their radical refusal to justify violence, Christians must not leave the smallest breach."[32] Although particularly clear in his discussion of violence, this reflects a wider feature of Ellul's approach to the task of Christian ethics. He is constantly on the alert to prevent a Christian ethic becoming a means of human self-justification that escapes God's gracious gift of justification by faith in Christ.[33]

Violence, Ellul argues, is a sign of the fact that humanity has sinned and ruptured our communion with God. We must not, therefore, formulate means to justify it in certain circumstances. Instead, we must confess our sin and seek God's forgiveness. For Ellul, the important truth is that the Christian cannot have a good conscience—"the Christian, even when he permits himself to use violence in what he considers the best of causes, cannot either feel or say that he is justified; he can only confess that he is a sinner, submit to God's judgment, and hope for God's grace and forgiveness."[34] It is important to realize that Ellul as emphatically rejects pacifist-inspired forms of self-justification which are developed for a policy of non-violence. He is quite honest that, "in the face of the tragic problem of violence, the first truth to be discerned is that, whatever side he takes, the Christian can never have an easy conscience and never feel that he is pursuing the way of truth."[35] Yoder is therefore right to describe Ellul as holding the view that "the Christian will have to use violence but will know that it is sinful,"[36] but

31. Ibid., 140.

32. Ibid., 141.

33. The fullest account of this is Ellul, *To Will and To Do*, 108, in which Ellul asserts, "Every honest reflection must absolutely begin by acknowledging that . . . there cannot be a Christian ethic." For further elaboration see Goddard, *Living the Word, Resisting the World*, 108–12.

34. Ellul, *Violence*, 138.

35. Ibid.

36. Yoder, *Nevertheless*, 177, note 16.

Ronald Ray is also correct in drawing attention to the fact that "even the Christian position of non-violence involves guilt."[37]

This approach to the question of a Christian attitude to war provides important challenges to some of the uses Christians make of the just war tradition. That tradition, in defending the use of force to combat injustice, can at times appear to lose sight of the fact that all war is always a sign of humanity's rebellion against and alienation from the God of peace. The best Christian defenders of just war acknowledge this and so O'Donovan opens his study with the need to hesitate over the achievement of just war theory because "the will of God for humankind is peace" and peace is the ontological truth of creation, the goal of history, and a practical demand laid upon us.[38] In contrast, the just war approach can too easily become a means by which "our side" in a military conflict seeks to claim moral superiority over the enemy and believe itself not guilty. Too many politicians and Christian leaders uncritically apply the "criteria" for a just war in a simplistic manner as a checklist of tests in order to show that the decision to go to war is justified and that right is on the side of their government. Ellul, in contrast, highlights the painful and tragic reality of living in a fallen world and being, in Luther's famous phrase, *simul justus et peccator*.[39]

There is, however, a major weakness in Ellul's approach. This is found in the fact that in its aversion to any form of self-justification his ethic is left being of little or no practical help to people faced with the harsh realities of living and acting in the real world. Two pieces of evidence show the dangers in Ellul's approach. Firstly, he appears incoherent and inconsistent when, despite his universal and sweeping categorizations and condemnations in relation to violence, he attempts to make moral distinctions between different violent acts. He will state that as a Christian he "cannot call violence good, legitimate and just" and yet there are situations when he says he approves of certain violent acts.[40] Indeed, in the original French, he even

---

37. Ray, *A Critical Examination of Jacques Ellul's Christian Ethic*, 196, note 3.

38. O'Donovan, *The Just War Revisited*, 1ff.

39. This element is present but often forgotten in the Christian tradition of reflection about war. It is seen, for example, in the medieval requirement for returning soldiers to do penance (see the brief discussion in Bell, *Just War As Christian Discipleship*, 44–45). A fuller discussion can now be found in Delahunty, "The Returning Warrior and the Limits of Just War Theory," 219–96.

40. Ellul, *Violence*, 133, 69.

writes of conditions in which the use of violence is acceptable and not condemnable.[41] Yet, later he can write that violence is always condemnable.[42]

Secondly, when it comes to the full and extreme horrors of war, we see the further difficulty that arises when treating all violence as the same and refusing to offer any means of moral discrimination. Here, Ellul appears to accept that "anything goes" once war has begun. This is in stark contrast to the just war tradition's desire to limit the use of force once war has begun, or *jus in bello*. Instead, Ellul appears to refuse any moral constraint least those who accept the proposed limits then believe they are justified in the limited violence that they do use. So, in conversation with Patrick Troude-Chastenet he reflected on the French experience in Algeria in these terms:

> According to me, once you have decided to go to war you have to go all out and use every means at your disposal. This is the case that applied in Algeria. Everyone was shouting their heads off against the torture that was going on. But the real problem was not the torture but the war itself. There is no morality in war. If you want to win you must pull out all the stops.[43]

The above demonstrates that Ellul is in a paradoxical situation compared to the just war tradition. That tradition seeks to limit war by acknowledging certain carefully delineated situations in which the use of coercion is justified and permitted and beyond which it is unjustified and absolutely prohibited. In so doing, it also lays down clear boundaries within military conduct and even a duty in certain contexts to sue for peace rather than to use immoral means. Ellul, in contrast, stands resolutely opposed to violence. However, his refusal to distinguish between different forms and levels of violence, his rejection of anything that could be construed as justification for violence, and his emphasis instead on the need to confess our necessary sinfulness in the fallen world, means that Christians guided by his approach are left unable to make important moral distinctions. So, in relation to the recent and current "war on terror," this insistence that all violence is violence and can never be justified leaves Ellul unable to distinguish and condemn some forms of interrogation of prisoners as torture. In rejecting any morality in war and seemingly accepting the need to use all necessary means to win, he is in serious danger of allowing the moral vacuum created by his abstention from discriminating moral judgment being filled by a

41. Ellul, *Contre les violent*, 170.

42. Ellul, *Les combats de la liberté*, 166.

43. Ellul, *Jacques Ellul on Religion, Technology and Politics*, 39.

purely consequentialist ethic where the end of victory justifies any means. As a result, Christians following his approach could end up participating in torture, extraordinary rendition, or even, presumably, genocide or dropping nuclear weapons as a necessary but unjustifiable response in a fallen world.

In short, Ellul has an aversion to any approach to moral thinking that he believes risks facilitating self-justification or denying the continuing presence of sin in all our actions. Pushed to an extreme, however, this makes his writing incapable of providing moral guidance or setting clear and realistic moral limits. As Oliver O'Donovan comments in his discussion of whether killing is a moral evil that we are bound at all costs to avoid and thus participation in war totally prohibited,

> The curious hybrid notions of "sin within the realm of necessity" (J.Ellul) and "responsible assumption of guilt" (H. Thielicke) capture dramatically the subjective moral tension which belongs to a decision of such gravity, but they leave the deliberative question in paradox and so seem to have more rhetorical than conceptual persuasiveness.[44]

Finally, a further major difficulty in Ellul's approach in relation to justification is evident in his startling claim that "apart from the inspiration of the Holy Spirit, the use of violence is always and *a priori* contrary to the will of God."[45] Here it seems, having refused all forms of violence, he suddenly allows for divinely inspired violence and hence something more akin to holy war (might one even say *jihad*?) than a Christian conception of just war. How one would discern the Spirit's inspiration to use violence is, sadly, left unelaborated. Certainly it cannot be described by reference to the divine calling of political authority to exercise judgment in pursuit of justice as in the just war tradition. Presumably any attempt to say anything more than he does would be to deny divine freedom and risk providing a means of self-justification!

Conclusion

Ellul and the just war tradition clearly approach the subject of moral judgment in relation to war from quite different perspectives. It is important

44. O'Donovan, "War and Peace," 655–56.
45. Ellul, *The Ethics of Freedom*, 406.

to recognize that it is these different approaches or paradigms which then largely shape their different conclusions.

In the light of the valid criticisms and cautions raised by Ellul but also the serious weaknesses in his own method, the challenge is whether or not a third way is possible. This could represent a chastened form of just war thinking in the light of Ellul's critique. In contrast to Ellul's work (where his attempt to reconfigure the Christian tradition by making "violence" the controlling concept risks distorting the structure of the tradition's account of morality in war) this would recognize and build upon the strengths of the just war tradition. Rather than just subsuming war under a strong account of "violence" and eschewing anything that could amount to self-justification this would provide a careful structured analysis of the key questions which must be addressed in thinking about going to war and conducting war: who is to wage war? Why should they have recourse to war? When should they do so? How should they fight? It would draw on the wisdom of the just war tradition to discern where significant moral boundaries lie in each of these areas.

In particular, like Ellul in his earlier writing, it would be based on the conviction that the structure and limits which must be placed on any use of destructive or lethal force are defined by the fact that just judgment is not only necessary but good and the divinely ordained task of government in a fallen world. It is therefore certainly true that "violence" is a sign of the fallenness of the world—Ellul's emphasis on this must not be ignored even if it needs to be tempered—but it does not follow that all recourse to violence is the same and so moral discrimination impossible. According to O'Donovan,

> The distinction between a moral and a non-moral evil can be rendered in terms of what is evil *as action* and what is evil *as suffering*. Not every action that involves the suffering of evil is an evil action. The non-pacifist tradition has represented the justified belligerent as suffering the evil of necessity, but not as doing evil.[46]

There is, for example, a difference between war in order to right wrongs (just cause) and war for self-aggrandizement, even if the latter is sometimes masked behind a claim that it is the former. There is a difference as well as a similarity between, on the one hand, attacking opposing armed forces and,

---

46. O'Donovan, "War and Peace," 655.

on the other, engaging in torture of prisoners of war or blanket bombing of non-combatants.

This approach would, however, need to remedy the weaknesses in the just war tradition that become evident in the light of Ellul's approach. In particular it must redress the tendency to be unrealistic about the nature of human violence. There has to be a challenge to the idealism about human control in the face of the power of violence that so often undermines just war thinking. Alongside the "micro" ethical deliberation about how to respond in a particular context, there needs to be a realistic and critical "macro" ethical analysis of the various historical, political, cultural and economic forces. These shape the contexts and produce the situations in which war is having to be considered as an option and often take over and drive the prosecution of war once it is started.

Perhaps most important of all, Ellul's critique has highlighted the tendency of the just war pattern of thinking to be hijacked for self-justification which masks the pervasiveness of human sin. The tradition could, however, be used as a more critical and prophetic tool. It would then raise before those holding political power and claiming to act justly the challenging questions of their own complicity in global injustice and their enthrallment to the powers of Technique and propaganda as they make decisions about war in the contemporary world.

As in so many spheres of his thought, Ellul's work on violence runs the risk of an "all or nothing" response. Those attracted to the just war tradition easily ignore him as of no practical relevance to the realities of international power politics. Those eager for a prophetic Christian voice can easily buy uncritically into his sweeping analysis of violence and his powerful rhetoric by dismissing the tradition as "casuistry" and "compromise." They then often find they are unable to offer guidance to those—including many Christians—who bear the terrible responsibilities of political authority. They can, as we have seen, even appear to see no difference between limited and excessive violence.

By recognizing the deeper divergences in method and focus between Ellul and the just war tradition and outlining both his strengths and weaknesses, it is, however, possible to draw on but go beyond Ellul's work. This could then enable the development of a realistic analysis of the nature of war today which builds on the majority Christian tradition Ellul himself once embraced in order to encourage a prophetic yet discriminating voice for those seeking to be faithful disciples of Christ.[47]

References

Aquinas, Thomas. *Summa Theologica Volume II Part II*. New York: Cosimo, 2007.
Bell, Daniel M. *Just War as Christian Discipleship*. Grand Rapids: Brazos, 2009.
Biggar, Nigel. *In Defense of War*. Oxford: Oxford University Press, 2013.
Dawn, Marwa. "The Biblical Concept of 'the Principalities and Powers': John Yoder Points To Jacques Ellul." In *The Wisdom of the Cross: Essays in Honor of John Howard Yoder*, edited by Stanley Hauerwas, et al., 168–86. Eugene, OR: Wipf & Stock, 1999.
Delahunty, Robert J. "The Returning Warrior and the Limits of Just War Theory." *Journal of Law and Religion* 15 (2014) 219–96.
Ellul, Jacques. *Anarchy and Christianity*. Translated by Geoffrey W. Bromiley. Grand Rapids: Eerdmans, 1991.
———. *Les combats de la liberte*. Geneva : Labor et Fides, 1984.
———. *Contre les violents*. Paris: Centurion, 1972.
———. *The Ethics of Freedom*. Translated by Geoffrey W. Bromiley. London: Mowbrays, 1976.
———. *False Presence of the Kingdom*. New York: Seabury, 1972.
———. *Histoire des Institutions Vol 2*. Paris: PUF, 1989.
———. *Islam and Judeo-Christianity: A Critique of their Commonality*. Eugene, OR: Cascade, 2015.
———. *Israel: Chance de Civilization*. Paris: Premiere Partie, 2008.
———. *Jesus and Marx*. Eugene, OR: Wipf & Stock, 2012.
———. *Prayer and Modern Man*. Translated by C. Edward Hopkin. New York: Seabury, 1970.
———. *Subversion of Christianity*. Translated by Geoffrey W. Bromiley. Grand Rapids: Eerdmans, 1986.
———. *The Theological Foundation of Law*. Translated by Marguerite Weiser. London: SCM, 1961.
———. *To Will and To Do: An Ethical Research for Christians*. Translated by C. Edward Hopkin. Philadelphia: Pilgrim, 1969.
———. *Violence: Reflections from a Christian Perspective*. Translated by Cecilia Gaul Kings. London: SCM, 1970.
Ellul, Jacques & Patrick Troude-Chastenet. *Jacques Ellul on Religion, Technology and Politics: Conversations with Patrick Troude-Chastenet*. Translated by Joan Mendes France. Atlanta: Scholars, 1998.
Glover, Jonathan. *Causing Death and Saving Lives*. London: Penguin, 1977.
Goddard, Andrew. *Living the Word, Resisting the World*. Carlisle, PA: Paternoster, 2002.
———. *When Is War Justified?* Cambridge: Grove, 2003.
Hauerwas, Stanley, et al., eds. *The Wisdom of the Cross: Essays in Honor of John Howard Yoder*. Eugene, OR: Wipf & Stock, 1999.
Konyndyk, Kenneth J. "Violence." In *Jacques Ellul: Interpretive Essays*, edited by Clifford G. Christians & Jay M. Van Hook, 251–69. Chicago: University of Illinois Press, 1981.

47. This issue is further explored in Goddard, *When Is War Justified?*

Marlantes, Karl. *What It Is Like to Go to War.* London: Corvus, 2011.

McMahan, Jeff. *Killing in War.* Oxford: Oxford University Press, 2009.

Neuffer, Elizabeth. *The Key to My Neighbor's House: Seeking Justice in Bosnia and Rwanda.* London: Bloomsbury, 2002.

O'Donovan, Oliver. *The Just War Revisited,* Cambridge: Cambridge University Press, 2003.

———. "War and Peace." In *The Blackwell Encyclopedia of Modern Christian Thought,* edited by Alister McGrath. Oxford, Blackwell, 1993.

Ray, Ronald. *A Critical Examination of Jacques Ellul's Christian Ethic.* PhD diss., University of St. Andrews, 1973.

Reichberg, Gregory M., & Henrik Syse. *Religion, War, and Ethics: A Sourcebook of Textual Traditions.* Cambridge: Cambridge University Press, 2014.

Reichberg, Gregory M., et al., eds. *The Ethics of War: Classic and Contemporary Readings.* Oxford: Blackwell, 2006.

Rognon, Frederic. *Une Pensee en Dialogue.* Geneva: Labor et Fides, 2007.

Storkey, Alan. *War or Peace?: The Long Failure of Western Arms.* Austin, TX: Christian Studies Press, 2014.

Yoder, John Howard. *Nevertheless.* Scottsdale, PA: Herald, 1992.

Chapter 4

Police, Technique, and Ellulian Critique: Evaluating Just Policing

Andy Alexis-Baker

SINCE THE ATTACKS ON the World Trade Center and the Pentagon on September 11, 2001, many pacifist-minded Christians have begun to explore differences between policing and warfare with the noble hope of limiting or even abolishing war as we know it. For example, Catholic theologian Gerald Schlabach has developed a theory he calls "just policing." Schlabach argues that the differences between policing and war are significant enough to merit a wholesale realignment of just war and pacifist thinking. Rather than justify war according to abstract criteria, just policing would draw upon international law to pursue suspected criminals, which should limit civilian casualties and the demonizing of individuals and groups.[1] If just war theorists would honestly explore these distinctions, they might recognize that policing is more appropriate to Christian duty than war. If pacifists would "support, participate, or at least not object to operations with recourse to limited but potentially lethal force," then a *rapprochement* might occur between just war theorists and pacifists through policing.[2]

In *God's Politics*, Jim Wallis claims that since 9/11 many Christians have re-read Jacques Ellul, "who explained his decision to support the resistance movement against Nazism by appealing to the 'necessity of violence'

1. Schlabach, *Just Policing, Not War*, 4.
2. Ibid., 3.

but wasn't willing to call such recourse 'Christian.'"[3] Similarly, Christian pacifists might respond to terrorism, Wallis claimed, by advocating that the international community create a global police force to deal with violations of international law and human rights.[4] Such a force, Wallis wrote, is "much more constrained, controlled, and circumscribed by the rule of law than is the violence of war, which knows few real boundaries."[5]

Wallis' suggestion that Ellul's works may help to formulate a response to terrorism, and that such a response ought to be "policing" raises the question of what an Ellulian analysis of policing might look like. Ellul was after all an anarchist and viewed the police as a manifestation of *technique*. In fact, his most famous text, *The Technological Society*, uses the police as an example of *technique* over thirty times. In what follows, I will use Ellul—rather than summarize his views—to critique just policing. Those who advocate for just policing have not adequately tested whether police are less violent because of the rule of law, nor have they generally considered the possibility that policing may in fact sustain or even worsen violence, not lessen it.

The Importance of History

At the outset of his book *The Technological Society*, Ellul decries the scholarly tendency to reduce *technique* to machines, stating that this "is an example of the habit of intellectuals of regarding forms of the present as identical with that of the past."[6] But the caveman's tool differs qualitatively from modern technology. This same bad habit applies to current reflections on police. Police have not always existed; they are a modern invention.

Greco-Roman cities did not employ officials to prevent or detect common criminal activity; citizens themselves performed these tasks.[7] Athenian law centered on private prosecution, which meant that the victim or the victim's family prosecuted the perpetrator in Athenian courts. For public crime like stealing city property, any citizen could prosecute and

---

3. Wallis, *God's Politics*, 166.

4. Ibid., 164–67.

5. Ibid., 166.

6. Ellul, *Technological Society*, 3.

7 For more on law enforcement in ancient Athens and Rome see Cohen, *Law, Violence, and Community in Classical Athens* and Nippel, *Public Order in Ancient Rome*.

would do the necessary detective work and witness solicitation.[8] Athenians usually settled disputes through negotiation, mediation, and arbitration with minimal formal structures or authorities and stressed keeping peace over placing blame. To Athenians, democracy meant "consensus rather than coercion, participation rather than delegation. At the judicial level, the principle of voluntary prosecution . . . was fundamental."[9] Far from pandemonium, the Athenian system worked well. A state police would have been unthinkable.

Roman society worked in a similar way. If a person witnessed a crime, they cried out for those nearby to help capture the perpetrator and aid the victim. The Roman military never involved itself in such acts unless a riot or rebellion was about to ensue that would disrupt the flow of goods to Rome. Classicist Wilfried Nippel claims, "We do not even know to what degree (if at all) the Roman authorities undertook prosecution of murder."[10]

This informal "hue and cry" system prevailed through the Middle Ages as see in Chaucer's "Nun's Priest's Tale." As Chaucer described it, the hue and cry involved shouting to draw attention to a crime. Those nearby gathered to witness, to help, to investigate and even to right the wrong. They might form a *posse comitatis*, led by the shire reeve (later called "sheriff") who was an estate manager, to hunt for a fleeing felon. The entire process was a community activity, not the responsibility of a professional police. This description is confirmed in legal codes throughout Europe. For instance, the municipal code of Cuenca, Spain, published around 1190 CE, describes city employees such as judges, an inspector of market weights, a bailiff to guard incarcerated individuals, a town crier and guards for agriculture. But the code does not mention any officials to detect or prevent crime. At most, medieval cities had night watchmen, who were not police but firemen who might also warn of other dangers.

The American colonies used the hue and cry and night watch system, memorialized in Paul Revere's night-time warning, "The British are coming!" The English-speaking world developed professionalized preventative policing during the nineteenth century. In America, these police forces evolved along two paths. Southern police forces evolved from state-mandated slave patrols, which monitored every aspect of slave life to prevent revolts. These armed patrols morphed into southern police forces before

8. Hunter, *Policing Athens*, 125.

9. Ibid., 188.

10. Nippel, *Public Order in Ancient Rome*, 2.

and after the Civil War. Despite occasional white protests, the police carried firearms because, they claimed, the shadowy fear of slave revolts and the mythical physical prowess of a revolting slave necessitated well-armed police.[11] Most southern police departments, however, formed postbellum, simply taking over slave patrol disciplinary methods and applying them to the newly freed back populations through arrests on disorderly conduct, public intoxication, loitering, larceny and prostitution. Born in 1868, American historian and social activist W.E.B. DuBois later said,

> The police system of the South was originally designed to keep track of all Negroes, not simply of criminals; and when the Negroes were freed and the whole South was convinced of the impossibility of free Negro labor, the first and almost universal device was to use the courts as a means of reenslaving the blacks. It was not then a question of crime, but rather one of color, that settled a man's conviction on almost any charge. Thus Negroes came to look upon courts as instruments of injustice and oppression, and upon those convicted in them as martyrs and victims.[12]

In the North, police departments emerged in the nineteenth century to suppress the "dangerous class." In city after city police departments combated working class vices such as drinking and vagrancy, not violent crime. For instance, from 1873 to 1915 police superintendents in Buffalo, New York consistently requested increased funding to hire more police, citing as a reason not a rise in violent crime, but labor strikes.[13] Arrest records confirm this focus. The 1894 records from Buffalo—then a city of 300,000—show that police arrested 6,824 people for drunkenness, 4,014 for disorderly conduct, 4,764 for vagrancy, and 1,116 for being tramps.[14] Yet they arrested only 98 people for felonious violence (murder, robbery and rape).[15] The superintendents—invariably tied to big businesses—used "public order" arrests alongside more violent methods to break strikes and control unions.

Besides maintaining class order, northern police also helped consolidate political power. The police controlled elections by promoting turnout, monitoring voting stations, and harassing electoral opposition to the current administration since new regimes usually replaced existing police with

11. See Wagner, *Disturbing the Peace.*

12. Du Bois, *Souls of Black Folk,* 145.

13. Harring, *The Buffalo Police,* 43.

14. Ibid., 201.

15. Ibid., 192.

loyalists. This happened following elections in Los Angeles (1889), Kansas City (1895), Chicago (1897), and Baltimore (1897).[16]

Understanding this history of policing is important. Do the police represent a natural desire for security that is central to all societies, dismissals of which reveal a profound naiveté? Or is modern policing a form of Ellulian *technique* that represents, according to Ellul, a profound shift in western history? My contention is that instead of promoting the common good or protecting the weak, police have historically promoted particular interests, siding with their employers and with dominant racial and economic groups. Police *technique* is applicable to many areas, as Ellul claimed. The police did not result from inevitable historical forces but from calculated moves to maintain social stratification that continue into the present.

The Rule of Law Is an Illusion

Besides mistakenly making the police into an ancient and natural institution, the notion that the rule of law restrains police violence unlike the military remains untested. For Ellul, the rule of law is a pure illusion: "We must unmask the ideological falsehoods of many powers, and especially we must show that the famous theory of the rule of law which lulls the democracies is a lie from beginning to end."[17] Taking this statement seriously, rule of law as it functions in just policing should be challenged at two levels. First, when the US military charges a soldier with a felony, such as abusing prisoners or killing civilians, 90 percent are convicted and most are incarcerated.[18] By comparison, in 2009 only 33 percent of American police officers charged were convicted—even if they killed unarmed, innocent people—and only 64 percent of those convicted were incarcerated.[19] These statistics contradict the assumption that the law moderates police behavior more so than that of the military.

---

16. See Fogelson, *Big-City Police*.

17. Ellul, *Anarchy and Christianity*, 16.

18. According to the 2009 "Annual Report of the Code Committee on Military Justice" 1,098 soldiers across all military branches were charged with the equivalent of a serious felony under military law. Of those, 972 were convicted.

19. The statistics on police misconduct are created by a Non-Governmental Organization called The National Police Misconduct Statistics and Reporting Project and are "low-end estimates" based on news reports across the United States.

More fundamentally, however, policing advocates have missed that police operate as a sovereign power that stands above the law through their discretionary powers whereby they determine when, where, and upon whom they will implement law. This discretionary power conflicts with western democratic theory, which gives pride of place to the rule of law. John Locke, for example, argued that "settled and standing rules" should circumscribe discretionary authority; due process should prioritize individual rights over coercive police powers; and the rule of law should protect citizens from arbitrary arrest and ensure their fair treatment while in custody, for "wherever law ends," Locke proclaimed, "tyranny begins."[20] Locke prohibited discretion as tyrannical except in emergencies where "the safety of the people . . . could not bear a steady fixed route."[21] At that point the executive could "act according to discretion for the public good, without the prescription of the law, and sometimes even against it."[22] Locke thus pushed discretion—a decision outside the law—to the edge of government, denying its necessity in quotidian governance.

Echoing Locke, Jeffrey Reiman argues that "police discretion begins where the rule of law ends: police discretion is precisely the subjection of law to a human decision beyond the law."[23] Because police operate in "low visibility" conditions, the only people likely to know that the police officer decided not to invoke the law are the police officer and the suspect. Thus discretionary decisions are unreviewable and risk becoming arbitrary and prejudiced, particularly in cases of racial profiling, police brutality and class bias. In using discretion, police act as sovereigns in a state of emergency and can disregard law. Thus the assumption that police operate under the rule of law ignores routine discretion that transforms the police from an institution that enforces law, into a sovereign institution that can act without lawful authority and even against the law.[24] The police are thus an autonomous form of *technique*.

20. Locke, *Two Treatises of Government*, 189, 90; Bk 2, §202.

21. Ibid., 169; Bk 2, §56.

22. Ibid., 172; Bk 2, §60. For a discussion of Locke's notion of prerogative see Pasquale, "Locke on King's Prerogative," 198–208.

23. Reiman, "Is Police Discretion Justified in a Free Society?" 74.

24. In the fictional HBO series, *The Wire*, which is a hard-hitting critique of not only current American policing, but other institutions as well, one of the seasoned police officers named McNulty tells his fellow officer: "Let me let you in on a little secret. The patrolling officer on his beat is the one true dictatorship in America. We can lock a guy up on the humble, lock him up for real, or drink ourselves to death under the expressway

In states of emergencies, sovereigns suspend law and use their monopoly on violence most often in police actions both externally and internally. Internally, the Holocaust was a police action within a state of emergency that Hitler had declared soon after his rise to power. During the Holocaust, the police did not violate German law; the entire operation was legal.[25] These states of emergencies are not confined to totalitarian states. The United States, for instance, has experienced nearly uninterrupted states of emergencies since the 1800's, using them to suppress labor disputes, deport "communists," and to execute people in the Civil War. Police actions are characteristic of sovereign power in times of national emergency, and this power has often been of the most brutal kind. These powers have been routine and are not exceptional at all, as Ellul argues,

> But so long as it faces crisis or encounters obstacles, the state does what it considers necessary, and following the Nuremberg procedure it enacts special laws to justify action which in itself is pure violence. These are the "emergency laws," applicable while the "emergency" lasts. Every one of the so-called civilized countries knows this game.[26]

Community, Policing, and Order

With discretionary powers, police primarily maintain order rather than enforce law. But, Ellul would remind us:

> This order has nothing spontaneous in it. It is rather a patient accretion of a thousand details. And each of us derives a feeling of security from every one of the improvements which make this order more efficient and the future safer. Order receives our complete approval; even when we are hostile to the police, we are by a strange contradiction, partisans of order.[27]

and our side partners will cover us. No one, I mean no one, tells us how to waste our shift!"

25. Other scholars have also noted that the Holocaust was legal and a police action. See Berenbaum, "The Impact of the Holocaust on Contemporary Ethics," 256. Quoting a Nazi official Hannah Arendt wrote, "only the police 'possessed the experiences and the technical facilities to execute an evacuation of Jews *en masse* and to guarantee the supervision of the evacuees.' The 'Jewish State' was to have a police governor under the jurisdiction of Himmler." See Arendt, *Eichmann in Jerusalem*, 76.

26. Ellul, *Violence*, 86.

27. Ellul, *The Technological Society*, 103.

The trick for police is to make people "partisans of order," and since the police represent order itself, we must see the police as indispensable. This is how community policing theory works.

Community policing theorists have long recognized the distinction between law and order and therefore promote broader discretionary police power, not less. According to Joshua Cohen and Joel Rogers, "'Community policing' combines greater police/community cooperation with increased police discretion."[28] For them, procedural rules and laws inordinately restrict the police to observing an individual's legal rights over the community's well-being. Thus ostensibly minor issues such as panhandling, loitering, and vagrancy remain unchecked but grow into larger problems as they signal lack of communal welfare to criminally-prone outsiders who subsequently invade the neighborhood. Community policing argues that police should have discretionary power to "clean up" these initial "disorders" even if their actions are not "easily reconciled with any conception of due process or fair treatment" and would probably "not withstand a legal challenge."[29]

The underlying premise of community policing bifurcates and simplifies community into "orderly" people (the community) and "disorderly" people (outsiders). It strips some people of rights and constructs a simplified community whose sole problems tend to be deviant outsiders and those inside who neglect quality of life issues like "broken windows." The very word "community" connotes positive images, and masks the contested and complex nature of real communities. Furthermore, community policing deploys the word *against* some people and advocates that police be permitted to use any means necessary to rid a "community" of these "disorders." By putting cops back on the beat and giving them a seemingly friendly face in the creation and maintaining of white bourgeois order, police do exactly as Ellul describes them in *The Technological Society*. They appear to protect "good citizens," relieving the citizenry of any fear and by patrolling openly lose their secretive aura, and therefore are not felt to be oppressive. Thus most citizens do not seek to oppose or escape police *technique* because the police have removed any desire to escape. That is the ideal of *technique*: to make itself invisible and internalized in its object.[30]

But to do this it has to exclude some people from the notion of community. Anybody who might cause "orderly" people to feel uncomfortable

28. Cohen, *Urgent Times*, xv.
29. Wilson, "Broken Windows," 35, 31.
30. Ellul, *The Technological Society*, 413.

must be stripped of liberal rights and chased out. They do not have to be violent, but in the words of prominent community policing theorists merely "disorderly people. Not violent people, nor, necessarily, criminals, but disreputable or obstreperous or unpredictable people: panhandlers, drunks, addicts, rowdy teenagers, prostitutes, loiterers, the mentally disturbed."[31] These are "broken windows" who if left unchecked will cause a spiral of crime and urban decay; indeed, they are the first signs of decay and must be eradicated with "zero tolerance" policies. This scapegoating mechanism has caused police to become much more violent toward these mere objects of police power.[32]

The Criminal Abstraction of the Technological Society

This scapegoating mechanism also reveals another problem in policing. From his experience working with gangs, Ellul argued that preventing youth from sliding into a life of violence "could not consist in adapting young people to society."[33] For Ellul, these youth were part of those "who do not conform to the level of efficiency society demands [and] are pushed aside."[34] Thus instead of helping them become professional bureaucrats, Ellul took "a stand against the technological society" and helped them become rightly "maladjusted" themselves. He saw that society's labeling of them as criminals and delinquents was simply part and parcel of the technological society.

More deeply, I think, the technological society must redefine such people as criminals and delinquents rather than enemies because criminality creates a permanent class of misfits to justify the state and its police. In just war thought—which, as a Christian pacifist, I am also against—enemies rightly construed have a political agenda that obligates the other side to treat them with a certain degree of equality and fairness. At war's end, people go home. And war ends eventually through some kind of negotiation. But once that enemy is redefined as criminal, terrorist, or delinquent, they are depoliticized. Instead of legitimate political claims, such people act out of insanity and hatred. One only needs to remember how those who planned the attacks on 9/11 were described and how no thought of

31. Wilson, "Broken Windows," 30.

32. Alexis-Baker, "Community, Policing and Violence," 104–5.

33. Ellul, *In Season, Out of Season*, 120.

34. Ibid., 129.

negotiation was countenanced to see that this re-labeling serves to create a permanent conflict and justify the state, including its police *technique*. The *technique* becomes much further entrenched and the violence more intractable with this shift in identity.

International War in Police Garb

A global police force will only quicken the march of the technological society and is really only a technical solution to technological problems. Ellul himself saw modern policing as a *technique* designed "to put . . . useless consumers to work."[35] Techniques intertwine into a system so that a *technique* applies across disciplines. So policing naturally carries over into economics. When the emerging capitalist system called for more laborers, the police were created to put non-producers to work, outlawing loitering, gathering firewood and other necessities from the commons, all of which made it harder for non-producers to stay outside the emerging economic order. Thus *technique* expands. The police are no exception. It seems naïve to suggest that the police would not expand into economic *techniques*, for example, on the international order. What would a broken window look like on the international scene? Who are the "panhandlers, drunks, addicts, rowdy teenagers, prostitutes, loiterers, the mentally disturbed" that are the human embodiments of broken windows when one's community is the whole world? If international broken windows must be addressed so that they do not invite a spiral of unrest and violence, who is to notice and fix these windows? In community policing theory it is an outside police force that aggressively drives out undesirable elements, often violating their rights in the name of community. It seems unfathomable that an international police force would not be used to expand global capital markets.

Looking Outside the System

As one example of a non-technical way of thinking about security we might look to the Paez tribe in Colombia, 100,000 people strong, who have completely disarmed their indigenous guard. This guard is not a professional force, but is made up of all volunteers and includes over 7,000 men, women and youth. They carry a three foot long baton decorated with various colors

35. Ellul, *The Technological Society*, 111.

as a symbol of their authority, not as a weapon. When there is encroachment on their territory they communicate via radios and many of them gather together to confront the intrusion and try to persuade them to leave (a hue and cry). This does not mean that such a decentralized, democratic, and nonviolent practice is always effective in warding off outside aggression: currently the tribe is facing increased pressure from both the government and the Revolutionary Armed Forces of Colombia (FARC) rebels with encroachment from both sides. However at times they have been able to persuade the rebels to back off and to release hostages. They provide security at great personal risk to themselves and their communities. This is not really "policing," in the normal sense of this word, but a communal practice of care and concern for communal well-being through resolving conflicts nonviolently.

Conclusion

Just policing advocates distinguish between war and policing in such a way that policing must necessarily be less violent than war. They have historically maintained social stratification and expanded into new areas to justify their existence and operate not under the rule of law, but under the assumption that they should create order, a subjective concept that looks different to a radical anarchist than to a police officer. I have tried to demonstrate the flaws in this argument. In the end, Ellul's statement on these distinctions holds true:

> We hardly need to point out how simple-minded the distinction made by one of our philosophers is between "police" (internal), which would be legitimate as a means of constraint, and an "army," which would be on the order of force. In the realm of politics these two elements are identical.[36]

References

Alexis-Baker, Andy. "Community, Policing and Violence." *Conrad Grebel Review* 26. (2008) 102-116.

Annual Report of the Code Committee on Military Justice. Online: http://www. injusticeeverywhere.com/?page_id=1588.

36. Ellul, *The Political Illusion*, 74–75.

Arendt, Hannah. *Eichmann in Jerusalem: A Report on the Banality of Evil*. New York: Viking, 1965.

Berenbaum, Michael "The Impact of the Holocaust on Contemporary Ethics. " In *Ethics in the Shadow of the Holocaust: Christian and Jewish Perspectives*, edited by Judith Herschcopf Banki, et al. 235–60. Chicago: University Of Chicago Press, 2008.

Cohen, David. *Law, Violence, and Community in Classical Athens*. New York: Cambridge University Press, 1995.

Cohen, Joshua & Joel Rogers. Preface to *Urgent Times: Policing and Rights in Inner-City Communities*, by Tracey Meares and Dan Kahan, xv–xvii. Boston: Beacon, 1999.

Du Bois, W. E. B. *Souls of Black Folk*. New York: Penguin, 1989.

Ellul, Jacques. *Anarchy and Christianity*. Translated by Geoffrey W. Bromiley. Grand Rapids: Eerdmans, 1991.

———. *In Season, Out of Season*. Translated by Lani K. Niles. San Francisco: Harper & Row, 1982.

———. *The Political Illusion*. Translated by Konrad Kellen. New York: Knopf, 1967.

———. *The Technological Society*. Translated by John Wilkerson. New York: Vintage, 1964.

———. *Violence; Reflections from a Christian Perspective*. Translated by Cecelia Gaul Kings. New York: Seabury, 1969.

Fogelson, Robert. *Big-City Police*. Cambridge, MA: Harvard University Press, 1977.

Harring, Sidney *The Buffalo Police—1872–1915: Industrialization, Social Unrest, and the Development of the Police Institution*. PhD diss, University of Wisconsin, Madison, 1976.

Hunter, Virginia. *Policing Athens: Social Control in the Attic Lawsuits, 420–320 B.C.* Princeton: Princeton University Press, 1994.

Locke, John. *Two Treatises of Government, and a Letter Concerning Toleration*. Edited by Ian Shapiro. New Haven: Yale University Press, 2003.

The National Police Misconduct Statistics and Reporting. Online: http://www.injusticeeverywhere.com/?page_id=1588.

Nippel, Wilfried. *Public Order in Ancient Rome*. New York: Cambridge University Press, 1995.

Pasquale, Pasquino. "Locke on King's Prerogative." *Political Theory* 26 (1998) 198–208.

Powers, James, trans. *The Code of Cuenca: Municipal Law on the Twelfth-Century Castilian Frontier*. Philadelphia: University of Pennsylvania Press, 2000.

Reiman, Jeffrey. "Is Police Discretion Justified in a Free Society?" In *Handled with Discretion: Ethical Issues in Police Decision Making*, edited by John Kleinig, 71–85. Lanham, MD: Rowman & Littlefield, 1996.

Schlabach, Gerald, ed. *Just Policing, Not War*. Collegeville, MN: Liturgical, 2007

Wagner, Bryan. *Disturbing the Peace: Black Culture and the Police Power after Slavery*. Cambridge, MA: Harvard University Press, 2009.

Wallis, Jim. *God's Politics: Why the Right Gets It Wrong and the Left Doesn't Get It*. San Francisco: HarperSanFrancisco, 2005.

Wilson, James Q. & George L. Kelling. "Broken Windows." *Atlantic Monthly* 249 (1982) 29–38.

Chapter 5

Cultural Interpretation of Cyberterrorism and Cybersecurity in Everyday Life[1]

Dal Yong Jin

Introduction

IN THE EARLY 2010S, cyber terror's footprints throughout the world are real and getting bigger. With the rapid growth of platform technologies, such as smart phones, search engines, and social networking sites, as well as the Internet, several parts of our society, including government agencies, financial corporations, and research centers are highly exposed to cyber terrors.[2] While the attacks of September 11, 2001 against the United States have reflected a growing use of the Internet as a digital and physical medium against terrorism, the Arab Spring movements in 2011 have raised a concern for the emergence of social media as a platform for both cyberterrorism and cybersecurity. As Jacques Ellul explained in *The Tech-*

1. This article is an expansion of the original which appeared in the *Ellul Forum* 32 (2003).

2. The best works on this topic are van Niekerk, "Analyzing the role of ICTs in the Tunisian and Egyptian Unrest; Shehabat, "The Social Media Cyber War," and Gamreklidze, "Cybersecurity in developing counties."

nological Society, one should be looking at technology in its sociological aspect because technology is not an isolated fact in society but is related to every factor in the life of modern man. Like Ellul, Clifford Christians observed, "technology is the distinct cultural activity in which human beings form and transform natural reality for practical ends with the aid of tools and procedures."[3] He argues that cultures are humankind's distinctive and immediate environment built from the material order by humankind's creative effort.

Therefore, many computer and security experts have looked at the issue of cyberterrorism in a new light in recent years. This chapter studies the development of the concept of cyberterrorism in cyberspace. In particular, it examines cultural aspects of cyberterrorism to ascertain its characteristics. This chapter discusses the specific question of the relationship between cyberspace and cyberterrorism, as well as several cultural aspects, such as the relationship between humans and technology, and privacy. Then it addresses the significance of cybersecurity for protecting our society from cyberterrorism. Finally, it analyzes the importance of cyber surveillance and discusses the function of encryption as a valuable cybersecurity tool in everyday life in a digital society.

Governments throughout the world have come to understand that terrorists and cyber criminals, such as crackers—reckless computer geeks aiming to crack codes, or bring havoc to computer traffic—are using today's information infrastructure to bring havoc to computer traffic and threaten public safety.[4] The number, cost, and sophistication of these attacks are rising at alarming rates, with aggregate annual damage worldwide now measured in billions of dollars. The September 11 attacks and the following cyber attacks in many countries have awakened the world to consider the real possibility of cyberterrorism.

While there are several significant cyber terrors in the early twenty-first century, the September 11 attacks especially point to cyberterrorism due to several relevant reasons. One is Osama bin Laden's networks and his use of the Internet to organize the attacks. He used laptops with satellite uplinks and heavily encrypted messages to liaison across national borders with his global underground network even before 2001. The other is the possibility of using steganography, a means by which one can hide messages in digital photographs or in music files but leave no outward trace

3. Christians, "A Theory of Normative Technology," 124–25.

4. Castells, *The Internet Galaxy*, 41.

that the files were altered. Osama bin Laden reportedly used steganography to conceal his messages for the September 11 attacks.[5] Likewise, during the Arab Spring movements, both the protesters and governments in Syria, Egypt, and Tunisia utilized social media, as a tool to either organize protests or to control these protests through information warfare.

Immediately following the September 11 attacks, many New York citizens could not use telecommunication and online systems for hours after the terrorist attacks due not only to overload but also destruction of the telecommunication infrastructure including that in the World Trade Center. This combination of physical and cyber destruction may be much more common in the future. Such threats existed before the September 11 attacks around the world, but the possibility of a significant attack, specifically, a combined cyber and physical assault, is being taken much more seriously since those events.[6]

The growing threat of terrorism, which has become one of the most significant global issues in the early twenty-first century, raises the specter of increased security risks for information managers ranging from the nuisance of Web site defacements to the possibility that systems could be targeted in conjunction with a physical attack to maximize disruptions. Computer and security experts fear that cyberspace could be terrorist's next target because they saw a clear warning in the terrorists' reliance on, and expertise in, information technology. It had become clear that the computer communication infrastructure, on which wealth, information, and power in our world depend, is highly vulnerable to intrusion, interference, and disruption. Naturally, cybersecurity measures have come to the attention of governments as the most significant method to protect society from cyberterrorism.

Cyberterrorism in Cyberspace

In the wake of the September 11 attacks, many scholars, computer experts, and government officials around the world quickly jumped to the conclusion that a new breed of terrorism is on the rise and that society must defend itself with all possible means. They understand that cyber attacks are sufficiently destructive to generate fear comparable to that of physical terrorism. Attacks that lead to death or bodily injury, extended power

5. Kolata, "Veiled Messages."
6. Thibodeau, "War against Terrorism," 12.

outages, plane crashes, water contamination, or major economic losses are examples. Before developing the concept of cyberterrorism, however, it is necessary to explain the concept of terrorism. Computer experts and government officials borrowed the definition of terrorism to explain cyberterrorism, though no one definition of terrorism has gained universal acceptance. Brian Jenkins, a former advisor to the National Commission on Terrorism, described terrorism as the calculated use of violence such as fear, intimidation or coercion, or the threat of such violence to attain goals that are political, religious, or ideological in nature.[7] The US Department of State defines terrorism as premeditated, politically motivated violence perpetrated against noncombatant targets by sub-national groups or clandestine agents.[8] Meanwhile, Noam Chomsky used the term terrorism as the use of coercive means aimed at civilian populations in an effort to achieve political, religious, or other aims, and he explains the World Trade Center bombing as an example of this kind of particularly horrifying terrorist crime.[9]

Many security experts borrowed these different definitions to explain cyberterrorism; however they cannot agree on one single definition on cyberterrorism because terrorism in cyberspace is difficult to define. Among these, Barry Collin, a senior research fellow at the Institute for Security and Intelligence in California, defined cyberterrorism as the convergence of cybernetics and terrorism.[10] Possible cyberterrorism targets, therefore, include the banking industry, military installations, power plants, air traffic control centers, and water systems.[11] Terrorist groups will become increasingly adept at exploiting information technology (IT) in a growing number of fields.[12] This implies that the computer communication infrastructure, on which wealth, information, and power in our world depend, is highly vulnerable to intrusion, interference, and disruption.[13]

In particular, as evidenced in Arab Spring movements in Syria starting in 2011, on the one hand all means of information communication tools, in particular, social media, have been harnessed by the revolutionaries in their

7. See Jenkins, *The Future Coverage of International Terrorism.*

8. See US Department of State, *Patterns of Global Terrorism Report.*

9. Barsamian, "The United States is a Leading Terrorist State," 19.

10. Collin, "The Future of Cyber-Terrorism," n.p.

11. Cyberterrorism 2001, n.p.

12. Lia, "Al-Qaida's Appeal."

13. See Castells, *The Internet Galaxy.*

attempts to bring about the downfall of the regime, but the Assad regime has also used social media platforms and applied surveillance technologies to fight back.[14] After analyzing civil movements in Tunisia and Egypt as parts of the Arab Spring, it appears the philosophy of cyberterrorism is that information and related technologies are an offensive weapon as well as a target; therefore, in the context of the cyberterrorism perspective, the plethora of cyber attacks has changed the dynamic of the combat at a large scale that has transformed social media platforms from social to political in order to achieve political gain.[15]

Cyberterrorism, which is also sometimes referred to as electronic terrorism, netwar, or information war, represents a new stage in that it occurs in and with cyberspace, and means an attack on the information structure and function. Examples of cyber terrorist activity include use of information technology to organize and carry out attacks, support group activities and perception-management campaigns. Depending on their impact, attacks against critical infrastructures such as electric power or emergency services could be acts of cyberterrorism. Attacks that disrupt nonessential services or that are mainly a costly nuisance would not be. In other words, the potential impact of cyberterrorism on private corporations and government agencies goes well beyond the traditional civil and criminal definitions of damage. The damage from cyberterrorism has not been viewed only in physical terms. In this regard, computer and security experts assess the probability of various types of cyber attacks, which will occur in the near future:

- Very likely: Electronic warfare is the threat feared most. It could come in the form of denial-of-service attacks, in which crackers overwhelm and disable Web sites with junk data. Other electronic attacks include computer worms and viruses—malicious computer programs that spread via the Internet and erase computer data or clog Internet traffic.[16] Online harassment such as harassing email, unsolicited pornographic pictures, and online stalking is also included.

- Likely: State-sponsored computer warfare is aimed at mainly the US although it targets other countries. Many countries have developed

14. Shehabat, The Social Media Cyber War," 2–3.

15. See van Niekirk, "Analyzing the role of ICTs in the Tunisian and Egyptian Unrest."

16. See "Experts Fear Cyberspace Could be Terrorist's Next Target."

asymmetrical warfare strategies targeting vulnerabilities in US computer systems. Because of US military superiority, the countries see electronic warfare as their best tool to puncture US defenses. As such, North Korea also targets South Korea and the US.

- Unlikely: The cutting of hundreds of fiber-optic cables—which carry Internet traffic between major hubs—knocks out portions of the Internet. Such an operation would require intimate knowledge of where key data hubs are, which only a handful of Internet firms know. It also would require a Herculean effort: most fiber cables are underwater or buried underground, so they are not easy to attack.

- Very unlikely: The bombing of Internet facilities, such as major data hubs, cripples the Internet. However, it is nearly impossible because the Internet resembles a cobweb of geographically dispersed facilities. For instance, in the United States, there are major routing hubs in Silicon Valley, Washington, Chicago, and Dallas.[17] Likewise, Ericsson world network is centered in Sweden, the Nokia world network is centered in Finland, and the NEC world network is centered in Japan.

As can be seen in this dichotomy, computer and security experts do not take seriously the connection between computer and physical attacks, i.e., attacks on human beings. Terrorists could coordinate a cyber attack with other forms of attacks against physical infrastructure, such as those on September 11. For computer and security experts, however, the main defense against cyberterrorism is to protect the information infrastructure. Cyberterrorism could be understood as a means to attack computer systems and infrastructure rather than to attack people.

Cultural Aspects of Cyberterrorism

It is generally recognized that technological decisions are made first, with ethical concerns only considered after they are developed. Throughout history, those who have been responsible for propelling technological advances forward have often denied their moral responsibility. In this frame of mind their solutions do not require any ethical reflection. In fact, many users of technology argue that technology is essentially amoral and an entity apart from values. According to Ellul scholar Clifford Christians, "the

17. Ibid.

first major contribution of the philosophy of technology is its critique of the prevailing view in technological regimes. Technology is presumed to be neutral, that is, technology seen in mechanistic terms as tools and products. Technologies are not value-laden but achievements of engineering."[18] The instrumentalists indeed point out that, if people use technology for destruction or pollution, as in the case of nuclear weapons and chemical pollution, it should not be blamed on technology, but on its misuse by politicians, the military, big business and others.

However, the historical emergence of a technological culture has made the issue of moral responsibility for technological development increasingly urgent because technology inevitably brings significant risks, as well as great benefits. Computers and cyberspace, in which cyberterrorism occurs, also brings about risks because they were not created by sheer act of will. Computers and the Internet indeed draw attention to the commercial, political, and military interests from the beginning. Therefore, it is indispensable to seriously consider the human and social aspects of cyberterrorism in cyberspace. In this light, cyberterrorism could be understood based upon the relationship between man and technology. It requires understanding the relationship between communications and control together because cyberterrorism affects the relationship between communication technology and the humans who handle it. As Norbert Wiener argued,

> Society can only be understood through a study of the messages and the communication facilities which belong to it; and that in the future development of these messages and communication facilities, messages between humans and machines, between machines and humans, and between machine and machine, are destined to play an ever-increasing part.[19]

Indeed, communication and control belong to the essence of a person's inner life, even as they belong to our social life.

Regarding the relationship between people and technology, cyberterrorism occurs when humans use potentially harmful aspects of the technology. Cyberterrorism occurs because some consider cyberspace as a zone of unlimited freedom, a reference grid for free experimentation, an atmosphere in which there is no barrier.[20] For instance, crackers try—without permission—to enter computer systems by breaking through security mea-

18. Christians, "The Philosophy of Technology," 727.
19. Wiener, *Human Use of Human Beings,* 16.
20. Robins, *The Times of the Technoculture,* 91.

sures. Breaking into a computer system with criminal intentions is illegal and a case for criminal prosecution.

Meanwhile, cyberspace is a geographically unlimited, non-physical domain, in which, independent of time, distance and location, transactions take place between people, between computers, and between people and computers. Unlike physical attacks, cyber attacks are carried out by people in the comfort of their own homes and can occur in more than one place at a time through cyberspace. Cyberspace enables terrorist organizations to plan attacks more easily on multiple targets and spread their own organizations over a larger geographic area. It is not closed, but open, in fact it is where we live every day. To cyber terrorists, distance is meaningless. The Internet provides them with the ability to be halfway around the world instantly, in many places at once, and have an army of compromised machines to do their bidding.[21]

In fact, one characteristic of cyberspace is the impossibility of pointing to the precise place and time where an activity occurs or information traffic happens to be. Space and time are intertwined in nature and in society, and space organizes time in a network society.[22] This is possible because cyberspace plays a fundamental role in altering the nature of information's production, distribution, and consumption by allowing radically greater amounts and speeds of information flow.[23] Since more and more objects are provided via digital facilities, they acquire forms of intelligence, can communicate with each other, and thus create a permanent virtual space in which time and space lose their absolute significance. The spaces of the physical and the virtual world are closely interconnected.

The number and damage of cyber attacks worldwide has been growing with the development of broadband (high speed Internet services) and smart phones in recent years. Broadband users are seen as being more vulnerable to attacks because their computers are always connected to the Internet. In particular, several East Asian countries, which are showing rapid growth of broadband, produce the most cyber attacks of any country apart from the US. Asian and Pacific Rim countries indeed produced 91 percent of all attacks during the fourth quarter of 2001. With the rapid growth of smart phone usage in the Asian and Pacific Rim region in the early 2010s, many security experts and IT policy makers are concerned

21. Robinson, "Physical Disaster Propels Cybersecurity Initiatives," 17–20.
22. Castells, *The Internet Galaxy*, 407.
23. Jordan , *Cyberpower*, 117.

about the emergence of new types of cyber crimes. In particular, North Korea has periodically been implicated in a variety of cyber attacks against corporate and government websites in South Korea and the United States.[24] Hackers from North Korea have continued to attack several key infrastructures, such as financial banks, broadcasting corporations, and government agencies of the US and South Korea from diverse locations since 2003.[25] North Korea's cyber infrastructure has served a small elite, largely for purposes of waging assaults against South Korea and the United States.

The next generation of terrorists will grow up in a digital world, with ever more powerful and easy-to-use cracking tools at their disposal. They may see greater potential for cyberterrorism than do the terrorists of today, and their level of knowledge and skill relating to cracking will be greater. Cyberterrorism could also become more attractive as the real and virtual worlds become more closely coupled with automobiles, appliances, and other devices attached to the Internet. Unless these systems are carefully secured, conducting an operation that physically harms someone may be as easy as penetrating a Web site is today. In other words, societies that apply many digital systems are extremely vulnerable to cyberterrorism. With relatively simple tools the key functions of such societies can be disrupted. Therefore, cybersecurity is the essential topic in current debates on new forms of the war on terrorism because the relationship between humankind and technology must be secure.

Cybersecurity in Everyday Life

Security risks in digital systems can be caused by totally unpredictable factors, such as earthquakes, floods, fires, and lightning as well as cyberterrorism. Security can also be threatened by electromagnetic signals that suddenly open or close electronic gates and doors or set electronic toys in motion.[26] However, the government and the business sector have not paid much attention to security until recent years. In the business sector, corporations have spent billions of dollars for electronic security; however, companies spent, on average, only about $250 for security measures out of every $1 million they spent on information technology in 2001.[27] At

24. Sang-Hun, "North Korea Sees South and US Behind Hacks," 7.

25. See Warf, "The Hermit Kingdom in Cyberspace."

26. Hamelink, *The Ethics of Cyberspace*, 116.

27. Lemke, "Cyber Terror a Certainty," 31.

the government level, the situation was not far different. For instance, the United States government spent $938 million in 2000 to protect federal computer systems.

Increased security concerns in the wake of the September 11 attacks have stimulated spending for cybersecurity. The US government sought about $4.5 billion in its 2003 budget request, which accounts for 8 percent of its information technology budget.[28] Meanwhile, the US government created the Department of Homeland Security for protecting the country from both physical terrorism and cyberterrorism in November 2002. The department would have about 170,000 employees and $37 billion budget. In addition, the US and UK homeland security teams are to hold joint exercises as part of efforts to prevent simultaneous cyber terror attacks on the two countries beginning in April 2003. As is well documented, this history of networked computing has attempted to illuminate how the interests of national security professionals and private industry—particularly technology companies—have influenced its governance.[29]

Alarmed by the September 11 attacks, government and security experts are clamoring for the world to craft better cyber defenses. They want tougher laws against crackers, more resources, and closer cooperation among agencies to thwart attacks. As noted, they worry that the threat of cyber attacks will grow seriously as business and government use the Internet more. They point out that society needs cybersecurity tools and control strategies for society's security. In fact, cybersecurity issues are so much an intrinsic part of everyday life today because most of our social encounters and almost all our economic transactions are subject to electronic recording, checking, and authorization. For instance, we unblinkingly produce passports for scanners to read at airports, feed plastic cards with personal identifiers into street bank machines, fill out warranty forms when we buy appliances, key confidential data into online transactions, or use bar-coded keys to enter offices and laboratories. However, the growth of electronic commerce and electronic recording has brought about several negative effects for society, such as property damage, and business disruption through online fraud. As Robins and Webster addressed, information is thought to be the key to a new phase of economic growth, but it also causes severe damage for today's information society.[30]

28. Berkowitz, "Cybersecurity: Who's Watching the Store."
29. See Hart, "The Insecurity of Innovation," for more on this.
30. Robins, *Times of the Technoculture*, 122.

As for computerized surveillance and security issues, one of the most important is encryption. Encryption is the art of scrambling messages to a predefined code or key and thus ensuring only those who know the key can read the message. Encryption technology empowers users to protect their digital property from unauthorized use because only the intended recipient—the key holder—can access the information. In particular, the public key approach is the most powerful method of authentication. Two sets of keys are used. In the public key system, one key is publicly revealed and the other is known only to the user. The keys are linked in such a manner that information encrypted by the public key can only be deciphered by the corresponding private key. Specifically, the public key (the product) is used to encrypt a message. A message encrypted with the public key cannot be decrypted with the same key; only the corresponding private key may decrypt it.

In conventional correspondence two devices are employed to ensure security and authentication. For privacy purposes, it is customary to place a letter within an envelope. But we want the intended recipient to know that we sent the letter, not some impostor. When we sign a letter, that signature serves to confirm our identity. This is exactly what occurs in public key encryption. By applying the recipient's public key to the message, we are assured that only recipients read it. As the significance of the Internet increases, encryption policy becomes more critical in transferring and protecting information. Under an open and non-secure Internet system, the issue of encryption places emphasis on security, authenticity, identification, and validation in information exchange. For instance, as an effort to prevent unauthorized access or modification and to secure Internet commerce, the US government indicates that a secure Global Information Infrastructure (GII) should incorporate the following aspects:

- Secure and reliable telecommunications networks.

- Effective means for protecting the information systems attached to those networks.

- Effective means for authenticating and ensuring confidentiality of electronic information to protect data from unauthorized use.

In order to ascertain the characteristics and merits of cyber surveillance, it is worth comparing cyber surveillance with electronics-based surveillance technology, such as Closed-Circuit TV (CCTV) technology. Electronic-based surveillance technologies are recognized as the primary surveillance technologies today. They are very useful tools in prohibiting some teenagers from entering shopping malls for shoplifting or displacing them from certain city streets. The recent growth in the use of the open-street CCTV system has been accompanied by a proliferation in the use of visual surveillance in a wide range of different institutional settings, including hospitals, schools, high rise housing blocks, and the workplace.[31] It is useful because cameras in public places may deter criminals. However, CCTV surveillance is not useful in cyberspace because it is not a cyber-surveillance tool that functions in cyberspace.

Closed-Circuit TV also raises concern about privacy. While CCTV is a useful tool for discouraging shoplifting in department stores, it also keeps watch over every customer without their permission. While some government agencies and businesses believe surveillance is more important than privacy in order to protect physical property and even life, privacy is actually part of the problem.[32] Hence, in many countries electronic surveillance is mushrooming; however, the sanctity of privacy has also been eroded by the increasing intrusion of surveillance technology. Although safety and security are important, privacy should not be sacrificed for society's safety.

In addition, electronic surveillance is not adequate to protect global data and money flows. As seen thus far, protecting global data and money flow in a digital society should be one of the main functions of surveillance and cybersecurity. As the global flow of technology, information, people, images and symbols rises in volume, surveillance should be employed to track and monitor these movements. More delicate and effective surveillance tools, such as high level encryption technology, become essential for protecting our lives and our property.

Unlike CCTV, encryption tools reduce threats to an invasion of privacy while protecting global data and money flows. Considering personal privacy, encryption applies to medical records, personal credit ratings, and spending histories. The problems of failing security need urgent solutions, in particular, for the success of digital trading. The combination of security, privacy, and authentication should make electronic commerce, whether conducted on private networks, the Internet or even in person, the preferred medium for financial transactions of all sorts. In fact, "the widespread use of encryption is necessary for safe financial transactions online."[33] More

31. McCahill, "Beyond Foucault," 44.
32. Lyon, *Surveillance Society*, 66.
33. Jordan, *Cyberpower*, 133.

importantly, strong encryption potentially hinders cyberterrorism because terrorists cannot interpret the message as easily as if they were unencrypted. Although some terrorists have some decoding skills, it is not easy for them to overcome the encoding skills of security experts. One of the most obvious signs of surveillance is the overhead "electronic eye" of the CCTV camera, and encryption is one of the most effective "cyber eyes" of cyberspace. With these forces behind it, strong encryption might be thought of as an essential element of cyberspace.

Conclusion

With the rapid growth of digital and social media in the early twenty-first century, cyberterrorism has become a common phenomenon. The next terrorist attack may be not physical in nature but could come through cyberspace to disrupt the communication infrastructure, including social networking sites, which may eventually greatly disturb people's daily activities. Cyber attacks on the military, economic, and telecommunications infrastructure around the world can be launched from anywhere in the world, and they can be used to transport the problems of a distant conflict directly to America's heartland, as well as other countries. In many countries, regional information warfare such as in the confrontation between North and South Korea, and the protesters and the governments during the Arab Spring, social media especially facilitates communications and provides a degree of command and control for both the protestors and the governments, therefore forming the basis for network-centric warfare.[34]

However, it is true that the impact of this risk to the physical health of humankind is still minimal, at present, although the current state of cyberspace is such that information is seriously at risk. Computers do not currently control sufficient physical processes, without human intervention, to pose a significant risk of terrorism in the classic sense. Therefore, a proactive approach to protecting the information infrastructure is indispensable for preventing its becoming more vulnerable. Computer-based security technology, in particular high-level encryption, is strongly needed for securing today's society from terrorist attacks. Encryption is essential to protect the telecommunication infrastructure. This has obvious advantages for users' privacy, and it deters the members of criminal organizations accessing

34. van Niekerk, "Analyzing the role of ICTs in the Tunisian and Egyptian Unrest," 1413.

secret communication. Surveillance and security are not simply coercive and controlling. They are often a matter of influence and persuasion. We are all involved in our own surveillance as we leave the tracks and traces that are sensed and surveyed by different surveillance agencies. Encryption is a non-coercive security and surveillance technique in cyberspace.

There are two important points that emerge regarding cybersecurity in Ellul's writing. On the one hand, as Ellul has argued, we need to comprehend that technology is part of our society, and

> every one of the human *techniques* is related to all other *techniques*. We must be on guard against attempting to isolate them. Human *techniques* are closely dependent on economic, political, and mechanical *techniques*, not only because of their origin and potentialities, but even more because of the necessity for their application. To neglect the technical context of these human *techniques* is to live in a world of dreams. They cannot be isolated in a pure state; and their means, tendencies, and results must be interpreted in relation to these others. If human *techniques* were ever to come into conflict with the others, they would inevitably lose out, for they would retain no real substance.[35]

On the other hand, Ellul also reminds us that the necessity of cybersecurity does not demand us to automatically admit the encryption and/or cybersecurity standards forced by the government. Instead, we need to carefully balance security issues, civil rights, and privacy. In the early twenty-first century, just as technological development has become an increasingly powerful and determining feature of modern advancements in virtually every field of our society, so it has triggered a virtually concurrent rise in the violence, destructiveness, and organization of terrorism.[36] In other words, "information technologies have been hailed for their emancipatory and decentralizing potential, but new risks and threats developed new challenges to the online ecosystem. Today, responses to these threats have reframed the status of the digital sphere as a locus of conflict, the more extreme form of which—the development of cyber warfare capabilities—can be seen as a military colonization of cyberspace."[37]

In conclusion, the recent concern surrounding cyberterrorism and cybersecurity has exposed how intimately the decision making in the

---

35. Ellul, *Technological Society*, 394.

36. Ibid.

37. Alves, "Jacques Ellul's 'Anti-Democratic Economy,'" 192.

development and governance of networked technologies relates to national security or economic arguments. How closely these positions align with civil liberty concerns will make all the difference in how much privacy and openness are built into these technologies by design.[38] Cyber terror and security have become part of our everyday lives. Everyday life has been conducted more and more in cyberspace in modern times, and this has strong implications for surveillance. On a daily basis, life in cyberspace entails surveillance in constantly increasing contexts. Examining this idea from an Ellulian perspective is one avenue available to help make sense of this phenomenon.

References

Alves, A. "Jacques Ellul's 'Anti-Democratic Economy:' Persuading Citizens and Consumers in the Information Society." *Triple-c* 12 (2014) 169–201.

Barsamian, David. "The United States is a Leading Terrorist State: An Interview with Noam Chomsky by David Barsamian." *Monthly Review* 53 (2001) 10–19.

Berkowitz, Bruce and Robert Hahn. "Cybersecurity: Who's Watching the Store?" *Issues in Science and Technology* (2003) 1–12. Online: http://www.issues.org/19.3/berkowitz.htm.

Hart, Catherine, Dal Yong Jin & Andrew Feenberg. "The Insecurity of Innovation: A Critical Analysis of Cybersecurity in the United States." *International Journal of Communication* 8 (2014) 2860–2878.

Castells, Manuel. *The Internet Galaxy: Reflections on the Internet, Business, and Society.* New York: Oxford University Press, 2001.

———. *The Rise of the Network Society: The Information Age: Economy, Society, and Culture Volume I.* Hoboken, NJ: Wiley, 2011.

Cho, Sang-Hun. "North Korea Sees South and US Behind Hacks." *New York Times,* March 15, 2013.

Christians, Clifford. "A Theory of Normative Technology." In *Technological Transformation: Contextual and Conceptual Implications*, edited by E. F. Byrne & Joseph Pitt, 123–41. Dordrecht, Netherlands: Kluwer Academic, 1989.

———. "The Philosophy of Technology: Globalization and Ethical Universals." *Journalism Studies* 12 (2011) 727–37.

Collin, Barry. "The Future of CyberTerrorism." Proceedings of the 11th Annual International Symposium on Criminal Justice Issues, 1996. The University of Illinois at Chicago. Online: http://www.acsp.uic.edu/OICJ/CONFS/terror02.htm.

Cyberterrorism. 2001. Online: http://searchsecurity.techtarget.com/sDefinition/0,,sid14_gci771061,00.html.

Denning, Dorothy. 2002. *Is Cyber Terror Next?* Online: http://www.ssrc.org/sept11/essays/denning.htm

Ellul, Jacques. *The Technological Society.* Translated by John Wilkerson. New York: Vintage, 1964.

38. Hart, "The Insecurity of Innovation," 2874.

"Experts Fear Cyberspace Could Be Terrorist's Next Target." *USA Today*, October 9, 2001.

Gamreklidze, Ellada. "Cybersecurity in developing countries, a digital divide issue." *The Journal of International Communication* 20 (2014) 200–217.

Jenkins, Brian. 1996. *The Future Coverage of International Terrorism*. Online: http://www.wfs.org/jenkins.htm

Jin, Dal Yong. "Beyond Cyber-terrorism: Cyber-security in Everyday Life." *Ellul Forum* 32 (2003) 8–13.

Jordan, Tim. *Cyberpower: The Culture and Politics of Cyberspace and the Internet*. New York: Routledge, 1999.

Hamelink, Cees. *The Ethics of Cyberspace*. London: Sage, 2000.

Kolata, Gina. "Veiled Message of Terror may Lurk in Cyberspace." *New York Times*, October 30, 2001.

Lefebvre, Henri and Donald Nicholson. *The Production of Space*. New York: New York University Press, 1991.

Lemke, Tim. "Cyber-Terror a Certainty, and Government is Most Vulnerable." *Insight on the News* 18 (2002) 31.

Lia, Brynjar. "Al-Qaida's Appeal: Understanding its Unique Selling Points." *Perspectives on Terrorism* 2 (2008). Online: http://www.terrorismanalysts.com/pt/index.php/pot/article/view/44/html.

Lyon, David. *Surveillance Society: Monitoring Everyday Life*. Philadelphia: Open University Press, 2001.

McCahill, M. "Beyond Foucault: towards a contemporary theory of surveillance." In *Surveillance, Closed Circuit Television and Social Control*, edited by Clive Norris, Jade Moran and Gary Armstrong, 41–65. Aldershot: Ashgate, 1998.

Robins, Kevin & Frank Webster. *Times of the Technoculture: From the Information Society to the Virtual Life*. London: Routledge, 1999.

Robinson, Clarence. "Physical Disaster Propels Cybersecurity Initiatives." *Signal* 56 (2001) 17–20. Online: http://www.afcea.org/content/?q=physical-disaster-propels-cybersecurity-initiatives.

Shehabat, Ahmad. "The social media cyber-war: the unfolding events in the Syrian revolution 2011." Global Media Journal: Australian Edition 6 (2012) 1–9. Online: http://connection.ebscohost.com/c/articles/90658968/social-media-cyber-war-unfolding-events-syrian-revolution-2011.

Thibodeau, Patrick. "War against Terrorism raises IT Security Stakes." *Computer World* 39 (2001). Online: http://www.computerworld.com/article/2583506/securityo/war-against-terrorism-raises-it-security-stakes.html.

US Department of State. 1996. *Patterns of Global Terrorism Report*. Online: http://www.state.gov/www/global/terrorism/1996Report/1996index.html.

Van Niekerk Brett, Kiru Pillay & Manjo Maharaj. "Analyzing the role of ICTs in the Tunisian and Egyptian Unrest: From an information warfare perspective." *International Journal of Communication* 5 (2011) 1406–1416.

Warf, Barney. "The Hermit Kingdom in cyberspace: unveiling the North Korean internet." *Information, Communication & Society* 18 (2005) 109–20.

Weiner, Norbert. *The Human Use of Human Beings: Cybernetics and Society*. Boston: Houghton Mifflin, 1954.

Chapter 6

The Nigerian Government's War Against Boko Haram and Terrorism: An Ellulian Communicative Perspective

Stanley Uche Anozie

Introduction

THIS CHAPTER APPLIES JACQUES Ellul's thought to the Nigerian government's war against Boko Haram, examining the war as a manifestation of "necessity." How is information about the ongoing war effort managed and how is propaganda applied by the government when communicating to the Nigerian people? How does Jacques Ellul's communicative perspective provide the critical consideration for communicating humanly and with dignity while pursuing the war effort? The central idea is on the indignity of using the power of communication as a propaganda tool to counter terrorism or in any war against an insurgency. The central concern is: does the Nigerian government subtly apply propaganda as a "politically motivated strategy for controlling a population?"[1] Reviewing the situation in Nigeria and applying Ellul's thinking on propaganda and communication will help us evaluate this question.

1. Marlin, *Propaganda and the Ethics of Persuasion*, 34.

Nigerian Government and Emerging Democracy

The Nigerian government has been waging war against terrorist organizations such as the militants who disrupted oil facilities in the Niger Delta. On October 1, 2010, during the Independence Day Celebration at Eagles Square, Abuja, the citizens in attendance were attacked with multiple bomb blasts.[2] Boko Haram was also active at this time. The Nigerian government's response to these attacks included propaganda techniques such as psychologically persuasive or motivated approaches to influence the Nigerian masses to respond against terrorism and compel their support for the government response. It became difficult to distinguish between facts and fictions, truths and half-truths, and misleading information regarding the war effort against terrorism put forth by the Nigerian government.[3]

In our age of information overload, and the use of misleading information to influence people, Jacques Ellul's thinking on propaganda critically questions a government's role in the use of information to manipulate the citizenry. The Nigerian government war against Boko Haram provides an example of propaganda applied precisely in this manner. Ellul demands that governments "communicate humanly in the age of technology,"[4] especially when technology makes propaganda so effective by reaching ever larger numbers of people instantaneously in a "world of falsehood, trickery, and deception."[5] Regardless of the Nigerian government's use of propaganda and persuasion, Boko Haram represents a genuine threat that must be addressed through whatever means necessary. One might ask, "What is Boko Haram's motif?"

According to Dr. Godwin Jeff Doki, Senior Lecturer at the Department of English at the University of Jos in Nigeria, Boko Haram "seeks primarily to establish a strict Islamic law in most of the semi-desert areas of West and Central Africa with spiritual headquarters in Maiduguri."[6] Many scholars have suggested different reasons for the establishment of Boko Haram, the adherents of which believe in the supremacy of Islamic

2. Anozie, "Human Rights and Terrorism," 206–22.

3. Ellul, *Violence,* 5. Ellul notes, "the state . . . must have the right to wage war."

4. The theme of the 2014 Jacques Ellul International Conference held at Carleton University and the Dominican University College in Ottawa, July 13–15, 2014, at which this paper was presented.

5. Ellul, *Technological Bluff,* 336.

6. Vanguard (Nigerian Newspaper) Monday, June 9, 2014. See also Audu, "The Almajiri Institution, Boko Haram, and Terrorism in Northern Nigeria," 192.

culture and civilization over any other form of civilization. We consider that view as noteworthy since "Islam is both a religion and a civilization, a historical reality . . . It is also a spiritual and metahistorical reality that has transformed the inner and outer life of numerous human beings in very different temporal and spatial circumstances . . . and historically Islam has played a significant role in the development of certain aspects of other civilizations, especially Western civilization."[7] The current trend identified in Boko Haram is not the last word in the ongoing interpretation of its motif!

Ellul and Propaganda

According to Randal Marlin, Ellul scholar and author of *Propaganda and the Ethics of Persuasion*, propaganda is defined as, "[T]he organized attempt through communication to affect belief or action or inculcate attitudes in a large audience in ways that circumvent or suppress an individual's adequately informed, rational, reflective judgment."[8] This definition describes what is going on with the people in charge of the media and publicity and public policy issues for the current Nigerian government. There is the conscious effort to manipulate and control public opinion in Nigeria.

Propaganda is not only about manipulation and control of opinions through the dissemination of lies and half-truths, and truth presented out of context. Even the relative accuracy of information can be used as part of propaganda in order to change people's opinion; however, propaganda is not only geared towards changing opinions. Propaganda is aimed at "intensify[ing] existing trends, to sharpen and focus them . . . to lead men to action . . . to prevent them from interfering."[9] Ellul explains that propaganda is "too oppressive and [used] to persuade man to submit with good grace."[10] It goes with mass media that is brought "under single control"[11] in order to prevent any multiple and confusing source of communication. For one to really control the agency of communication, every other channel of 'divisive' communication must be under check. The information provided to the people is vetted for 'well-directed' consistency.[12] This well-

7. Nasr, *Islam*, xi.

8. Marlin, *Propaganda and the Ethics of Persuasion*, 22.

9. Ellul, *Propaganda*, vi. (See Preface by Konrad Kellen).

10. Ibid., xviii.

11. Ibid., 102.

12. Marlin, *Propaganda*, 22. Marlin describes it as well-intentioned propaganda.

directed consistency and control are aimed at the populace. Without the populace the purpose of propaganda is not complete or comprehensive. Ellul adds, "no propaganda can exist unless a mass can be reached and set into motion."[13]

The masses in Ellul's analysis consist of the poor or, the wretched of the earth, as Frantz Fanon would say. But these poor people are not so easily controlled or manipulated. In other words, one's socio-economic status determines one's accessibility or availability to effective propaganda. Ellul explains that "[M]odern integration propaganda cannot affect individuals who live on the fringes of our civilization or who have too low a living standard."[14] There is that paradox which rather points to the accessibility of the rich and relatively independent to the influence of propaganda.

This interesting paradox confirms the level of influence of propaganda. As Ellul notes about developed/developing countries and effective propaganda, "the ascent to that level is gradual, the rising living standard in the West, as well as in the East and in *Africa* makes the coming generations much more susceptible to propaganda."[15] It is through propaganda that "facts become known and attention to certain questions is aroused."[16]

Propaganda and Credible Information

In Ellul's view, propaganda is an essential aspect of communication in contemporary society. Another facet of the new technologies is man's predilection for "facts," which Ellul suggests modern man worships. According to Randy Kluver, in light of Ellul's comment on propaganda as *an inescapable necessity*, "those responsible for public discussions of issues such as the media systems and the government, now use the techniques [17]of propaganda to override rational discourse and critical thinking."[18] In this way, propaganda has the meaning as a negative technique of control and influence so as to disarm the capacity of constructive thinking.

Ellul ascribes a neutral character to propaganda. It can be used for either good or for evil. It reflects the motives and the objectives of the

13. Ellul, *Propaganda*, 104.

14. Ibid., 105.

15. Ibid., 106.

16. Ibid., 113.

17. Ellul, "The Ethics of Propaganda, 159–75.

18. Kluver, "Jacques Ellul: Technique, Propaganda, and Modern Media," 100.

individuals who are wielding the propaganda. The negative use of propaganda is very inimical to the value of facts and truth. Ellul further explains that this form of propaganda aims at the destruction of "truth and freedom . . . no matter what the good intentions or the good will may be of those who manipulate it."[19] In the end, the manipulation of information is accomplished through what *appears as facts* and credible. Whether propaganda is used for negative or positive reason, being credible and believable must be one of the conditions of its effectiveness. However, any propaganda, no matter how credible and effective it is, ceases when it stops.[20]

For propaganda to be effective, it must be based upon important or significant information. Serious propaganda cannot be based upon frivolous or unimportant information. Ellul notes that "propaganda to politically ignorant groups can be made only if preceded by extensive, profound, and serious information work."[21] The information used in manipulating or eliciting an expected response from the people should be credible. When the information is not-believable or non-credible, it reduces the quality of the propaganda and its influence on the people. According to Ellul, "information provides the basis for propaganda but [also] gives propaganda the means to operate."[22] Propaganda feeds on data, information, and images, and is most effective when the goal is to exert control over some segment of the populace. It is "the attempt to affect the personalities and to control the behavior of individuals towards desired ends," and these ends must be attainable.[23]

It is important to examine the classes within society that are most often the victim of propaganda. Not all people are easily subjected to effective propaganda. Some have more proclivities to becoming targets or victims of propaganda than others. The seemingly disinterested or passive crowd is usually among those most easily swayed by propaganda. The educated members of society could also become victims of propaganda. The public, Ellul affirms, "is just an object . . . that one can manipulate, influence, and use."[24] In the above, propaganda is not necessarily seen as bad but a

19. Ellul, *Propaganda*, 257.

20. Ibid., 296.

21. Ibid., 113.

22. Ibid., 114.

23. Glander, *Origins of Mass Communications Research During the American Cold War*, 22.

24. Ibid., 118.

technique that could be used to present a different social need and create the relevant awareness about issues of national importance.[25] It is in this sense of recognizing the good effect desired in using propaganda that our paper calls for true consideration of communicating humanly (even under the pressure of an exacerbating and destructive war against terror).

Ellul holds that "one cannot determine with any degree of accuracy how many people are being reached by a propaganda campaign."[26] Propaganda's effect is continual and advances among the various spheres of the community. Public opinions, perceptions, and the prevalence of facts, are all factors in understanding how effective propaganda has become. At times people who are under the influence of effective propaganda live in denial of this influence, especially when the facts used in distortions are believable, but when facts are no longer credible then propaganda becomes ineffective or inefficient. This is the case in the Nigerian government's war against Boko Haram.

Boko Haram and the Nigerian Government: Propaganda and the Crisis of Information/Communication Management

In the section above, we were not dealing with issues that are probable, but rather issues that are believable or credible. In Ellul's comment on indoctrination, which is a form of propaganda, he states, "as soon as the individual has been indoctrinated with the 'truth,' he will act as he is expected to act, from the 'spontaneity' of his conscience. This was the principle aim of propaganda in Hitler's army."[27] Ellul observes that "without this need for propaganda experienced by practically every citizen of the technological age, propaganda could not spread . . . there is a citizen who craves propaganda from the bottom of his being and a propagandist who responds to this craving."[28] People consciously, and some unconsciously, work together for propaganda to be effective.

---

25. Ibid., xviii.

26. Ibid., 262. See also Lasswell, *World Revolutionary Propaganda*, chapter 11.

27. Ellul, *Propaganda*, 120.

28. Ibid., 121.

Media Empire and the Defense of Powerful Interests

There is, as is common knowledge, the oligopoly and monopoly of our media houses.[29] Certainly, in many countries, some media houses serve the interests of powerful individuals and sympathetic governments. The recent incidents in Nigeria in terms of National Newspapers and Public Television corporations serving the interests of the ruling government open our minds to the power of government in the developing democracies to influence their people through media outlets. Ellul observes, "[T]o make the organization of propaganda possible, the media must be concentrated, the number of news agencies reduced, the press brought under single control"[30] By this he means psychological control. Let us look at the use of 'technique' to explain the nature of this psychological influence.

La Technique does not exactly translate into English as "technique" or "technology." *La technique* is about the mode of consciousness inherent in over-dependence on technical means. It refers to a self-directing and self-augmenting social process. Kluver explains, "Ellul does not argue against technique or technology itself, but rather the human mindset that replaces critical moral discourse with technological means and values."[31]

Many people have the understanding that technology has changed the world and almost everything about the world. In that sense, people are easily influenced through the power of technology in terms of information dissemination, manipulation, and influence on one's perceptions. Ellul notes, "the technical phenomenon is the main preoccupation of our time; in every field men seek to find the most efficient method."[32] Considering the prevalence of the use of propaganda through the media, from an Ellulian perspective, Kluver observes that the mass media (radios, movies, newspapers or newsprints) has become the "means by which collective life is lived and the collective consciousness is shaped. Moreover, the centralized nature of the mass media means that rather than encouraging thought, the media instead have been a crippling force of social control."[33] The end of propaganda is not making people understand but to psychologically

---

29. One has to recall the monopoly influence that the *New York Times* and *Wall Street Journal* have in the world and in general the American news media.

30. Ellul, *Propaganda*, 103.

31. Kluver, "Jacques Ellul: Technique, Propaganda, and Modern Media," 99.

32. Ellul, *Technological Society*, 21.

33. Kluver, 101.

compel them into "compliance."[34] The propagandist is not interested in people accepting his/her views. He or she is interested in compelling the people into following 'fixed' trends or 'pre-determined' patterns of behavior. Propaganda seeks people's response, not necessarily their agreement. Ellul adds, "[T]o the extent that propaganda rests on a contempt for man viewed as an object to shape and not as a person to respect, this signifies that the cause defended by propaganda implies a degradation of man, the impossibility of his acceding to his majority, to his personal responsibility, and that propaganda is evidently a negation of a freedom."[35] In other words, people lose the ability to individually decide or make judgements or be more creative in dealing with information.[36] We now take a look at how this information and communication technology is being used by the Nigerian government to control the masses in relation to their war against Boko Haram.

Propaganda Forces: Media Control in Nigeria

How do we communicate and how have we used information technology in influencing other people's thought and views? How has spin factor been used in leadership/governance in Nigeria? What is the role of the private media establishments and federal institutions such as Nigerian Television Authority (NTA), Nigerian Television Authority International (NTA international), African Independent Television (AIT, private media) in constructing the "psychological framework" that the government wants—and a framework consistent with Ellul's technological society? African Independent Television is owned by High Chief Raymond Dokpesi (Daar Communications), a close friend of the current President Goodluck Jonathan. Dokpesi was involved with supporting democratic progress in Nigeria in the 1990s. It was the first privately owned Television network and was also said to be Africa's first satellite television station. He also owns the first private radio station called Raypower FM Nigeria. It is unfortunate that most media organizations start off good but degenerate to become propaganda machines of any ruling government in order to receive largesse and contracts from government. This situation affirms the case of lack of integrity

34. Ibid.

35. Ellul, "The Ethics of Propaganda," 159–75.

36. Kluver, "Jacques Ellul," 103. Kluver also notes that propaganda sends a totalizing effect on the masses by disallowing "true competitive discourse," 104.

and consistency in objective journalism in Nigeria. Propaganda as we recall is about justification of self rather than explanation of the situation or reality. Public institutions at the charge or care of the federal government have now become tools of propaganda in the hands of serving leaders. This situation could be seen in the use of the federal military and police to intimidate the opposition parties during elections or to use them to support exclusively the interests of the ruling party. Considering the financial pressure that some of these independent media organizations go through to continue to be in business, some of them have now closed down, and those still around are playing safe to avoid being clamped down by government agencies or hunted down through indirect intimidations.

One recalls the case of the media organization called *Next 234*, owned by Dele Olojede. He had experience in journalism, working at *Newswatch* Magazine and *Sunday Concord* Newspaper as a reporter. The reports he wrote for the New York *NewsDay* some years ago on Rwanda genocide won him a Pulitzer Prize in 2009 and other accolades around the world. Despite these awards and accolades, his media organization failed to stay in business. *Next 234* began with the purpose of distinguishing itself in quality journalism/communication, in publication of hard facts without distortion, false-reporting, and manipulative propaganda.

Propaganda and Democracy (Propaganda, Nigeria, and Ellul)

Boko Haram's terrorist acts started as an agitation against violent executions of their members and a perception that the Nigerian government was abusing their fundamental human rights. Many considered the rise of Boko Haram was a result of poverty and abandonment of the poor masses in northern Nigeria. The young people needed jobs—sustainable ones—to escape from poverty. We believe that if enough economic opportunity were provided to the Niger Delta militants, and if these opportunities were extended to the unemployed youth in the north, some of them might not have chosen to support Boko Haram, or attempted to associate with Al Qaeda, or contacted Islamic State of Iraq and Syria (ISIS or ISIL).[37] As we are

---

37. Monica Mark has tried to associate Boko Haram and ISIS. ISIS had suggested that kidnapping girls in Chibok is similar to kidnapping and selling the Yazidi women into slavery.

seeing, unemployment can become "fatal when not controlled,"[38] and this is seen through the unemployed youth getting involved with terrorist groups like Boko Haram. There has been a serious barrage of inconsistency coming from Nigeria's leadership and spokespeople with regard to the direct relation between insecurity and unemployment.

The inconsistencies in explaining the relation between security and youth employment policies in Nigeria, especially in the recent government, is a pointer to what Adebayo Oyebade stated in his article: "Reluctant Democracy: The State, The Opposition, and the Crisis of Political Transition, 1985–1993."[39] The flip-flop nature of Nigerian practice of democracy shows serious lack of determination to change the way things are going, especially in the recent attacks. Ellul would consider this as a result of the lack of the ability to communicate especially when confronted by daunting situations: terrorism and insecurity problems in various Nigerian states.

In the situation above, the Nigerian state itself seems to become an abstract concept. As we know, a democratic state may not exist in reality. It could be just a mere concept with fictitious essence; unreal or imaginary as well as false; an empty, dead and cold concept. When the values and principles that a state should maintain are not considered important, then Ellul considers such a state at this point, to be a failing state. Without a doubt, a citizen of a state could choose (not necessarily imposed by government) the above mentioned situation because of being susceptible to a visionless existence and also fall unto "propaganda of his choice."[40] Technically speaking, each member of a socio-economic category could fall within the reach or is targeted by a specific form of an effective propaganda. In this case, as Ellul explains, propaganda "has precise objectives, it does not concern just anybody. To analyze whether such selective propaganda is effective, it would be necessary to analyse only the target group or the particular that was to be modified."[41] Society or a community of people and individuals are the targets of propaganda, political illusions and distorted leadership.[42] There is an avalanche of myths of economic successes, hair-splitting political illusions,

---

38. See Okolo, *Squandermania Mentality.*

39. Oyebade, "Reluctant Democracy," 137–62.

40. Ellul, *Propaganda*, 104.

41. Ibid., 270.

42. Ellul, *Jacques Ellul on Politics, Technology and Christianity*, 15.

and structural oppression as Nigerians head to the 2015 elections in the midst of propaganda soaked political campaigns.[43]

In an election year in Nigeria, Ellul's observation that some political campaigns are forms of modern propaganda is not difficult to discern. [44] His definition of propaganda is very comprehensive in that it includes all aspects of the act of influencing people's attitudes. He considers propaganda as "a set of methods . . . to bring about the active or passive participation in its actions of a mass of individuals, psychologically unified through psychological manipulation, unified, and incorporated in an organization."[45] According to Ellul, the use of propaganda brings the propagandist and the propagandee into close contact. This unhealthy contact is the basis for profound psychological influence in a democratic society. [46] He notes, "[A] man who lives in a democratic society and who is subjected to propaganda is being drained of the democratic content itself—of the style of democratic life, understanding of others."[47] Propaganda can take away or help erode our democratic values. As we noted above, when a democratic state becomes a mere concept, a fictitious essence, it loses purposefulness, and becomes the myth of democracy. In that case it is possible for "the citizen . . . [to] repeat indefinitely 'the sacred formulas of democracy' while acting like a storm trooper."[48]

For the people within a democratic society, it is difficult to discern this wilful degeneration of democratic values because of the impact of propaganda. Propaganda, effective propaganda, takes root gradually. Propaganda aims at modifying the content of an opinion or "change[s] majority views, or destroy[s] the morale of an enemy."[49] The enemy—the citizenry—is the target of the information onslaught of the propagandists. It is a psychological warfare in which the citizens are turned into citizens of totalitarianism. If some of the people do not accept the policies of those in government,

43. I discussed this in my article on how governments support or sponsor structural terrorism to intimidate the masses. This also applies in the use of violence to compel people into accepting a manipulative approach in governance and information control or distortions. See Anozie, "Human Rights and Terrorism: The Niger Delta Oil War," 218–22.

44. Marlin, *Propaganda and the Ethics of Persuasion*, 36.

45. Ellul, *Propaganda*, 6, 61.

46. Ellul, *Violence*, 123.

47. Ellul, *Propaganda*, 256.

48. Ibid. See also Ellul, *Violence*, 97.

49. Ibid., 259.

then they are classified among the opposition (lovers of bad news) and enemies of government. Here is Ellul's explanation. Propaganda could be about
auto-justification. It provides its own morality and justification. When self-
justification is the basis for action then it manifests or creates the monster of
totalitarianism. Anyone who is against or outside this totalitarian ideology
or community is an enemy of the state. 'We' against 'them'! This situation is
encouraged through information distortion and manipulation.

Avoidance of misleading information is helpful to finding some
peaceful solutions in a civilised democratic society. For the current situation in Nigeria the questions are: what does government know? Are there
suppressions of news or information? President Jonathan's Special Adviser
on Media and Publicity—Dr. Reuben Abati— has applied some distortions
and media-myth strategy in his services to the president. This is same with
President Jonathan's Senior Special Assistant on Public Affairs (Special Adviser on Public Affairs)—Dr. Doyin Okupe— in his BBC interview with
Stephen Sackur on the Nigerian government and the rescue of the Chibok
Girls.[50] Okupe used the myth of propaganda by incessantly saying that "we
[the Nigerian government] always get it right."[51] We understand this in
light of Ellul's description of 'myths of hero', 'myth of happiness' and 'myth
of a great nation' such as the myths of peace, freedom, progress, etc.[52] It
means that the great 'hero' leader (President *Goodluck* Jonathan) will bring
happiness and '*goodluck*' as his good name implies![53] Okupe suggested that
the President's inability to visit Chibok and the volatile Northeastern states
was purposely shelved because of other urgent national issues. President

50. There are other members of President Jonathan's propaganda machinery but I
have chosen to focus on the most prominent ones, but that does not mean they are the
most effective and most important propagandists in this aspect of governance. I have
purposely avoided discussing names like Reno Omokri (effective with media technology
propaganda, using Facebook, the blogosphere, Twitter, etc). He is Special Assistant to
President Jonathan on New Media.

51. I associate Dr. Doyin Okupe's comment to a form of propaganda. Many people
are of the view that Okupe knows that the best thing for him is to keep fighting for his
pay checks. This situation is similar to the one described by Louis Lochner, the bureau
chief of the Associated Press in Berlin in the 1930s, about how journalists are controlled.
Lochner stated the policy of the German government as, "[T]o tell no untruth, but to
report only as much of the truth without distorting the picture, as would enable us to
remain at our posts (The comment is related to excerpts from Halton, *Dispatches from
the Front*.)

52. Ellul, *Propaganda*, 39–40.

53. Marlin, *Propaganda and the Ethics of Persuasion*, 34. Marlin describes them as
"useful myths in the minds of a population."

Jonathan finally made a surprise visit to Maiduguri on the 15th of January, 2015. Some political analysts are of the view that it was a good idea to visit Borno State before the actual political campaign stopover in some of the Northeastern States. Meanwhile, the President is yet to visit Chibok where the kidnapping of 219 girls took place. As Ellul suggests these myths provide people with false hope through captivating and "activating images."[54] It is simply undeserving and flattering for the success of the Nigerian society/people to be based on unfounded hopes, miracles and mere *good-luck* charms in order to influence public opinion. In fact, for Ellul, as long as there is propaganda, there is no genuine public opinion.[55] We think that the opinion about the real reason for the President not visiting Chibok has since fortunately changed.

Fortunately, contrary to Okupe's BBC suggestions and responses, Jonathan himself acknowledged, several months later, that Boko Haram had prevented him from going to places he would have loved to visit, especially the communities/victims of these senseless attacks.[56] One would like to think that President Jonathan had no other options than to acknowledge that the terrorists hindered his visit (he somehow will gain some sympathy votes against Boko Haram and the main Opposition party). It could also mean he is certain that the effects of propaganda on the Nigerian masses are weakening so he prefers to be honest as a way out of failing propaganda. In this context Ellul observes, "[A]ll propaganda evaporates progressively when it ceases."[57] In many different times the federal government and some presidential spokespersons are numbed to learn that the Chibok girls' saga is almost a sudden-death case for their party (PDP). Their propaganda—to influence public opinion—by claiming that the Chibok secondary school girls will be back before Christmas 2014 is already flat and ineffective since the arrival of New Year 2015.

Let us take a look at the failure of propaganda in Nigeria's war against terrorism. This failure was systemically exposed by the Chibok girls' kidnap and the series of propaganda crises that followed.

54. Ellul, *Propaganda*, 31–32.

55. Ellul, *Jacques Ellul on Politics, Technology and Christianity*, 15. Ellul holds this position by implying that there was no public opinion before Pierre Bourdieu.

56. See Lekan Adetayo, "Boko Haram restricts my movement-Jonathan" in *Punch Newspaper*, June 28th, 2014.

57. Ellul, *Propaganda*, 296.

Chibok Girls' Kidnap: Defence through Propaganda by Okupe

The failures to lead the Nigerian people with true, consistent facts after the kidnap have left the current leadership with a serious work of convincing the citizenry about government's commitment to democratic values and security, and support the achievement of common well-being for all the Nigerian people.

Okey Wali, the president of the Nigerian Bar Association, criticised the Nigerian government's weakness of leadership and inefficiency in communication in the face of terrorism. Mr. Wali noted that the Nigerian government's war effort is so far not yielding results. He asserts that the government needs to speak with facts and stand by the facts. It should not attempt to politicize the war effort against terrorism. Indiscreet party politics must be avoided in addressing such issue of national importance or emergency.[58] As an emerging democracy, we have to avoid the politicization and trivialization of urgent national problems and work together to address this security and corruption problem.

Let us now take a look at some of the inhumane and indiscreet propaganda and politicization/politicking with life-threatening terror war in Nigeria. Propaganda, for Ellul, is a consistent part of every aspect of the public life. It destroys the citizen's capacity for individual constructive discernment. In this light, Okupe's recent comments on BBC insinuated that the war by Boko Haram militants was because of the religious difference and ethnicity of the President. According to Jibrin Ibrahim, a political analyst at the Centre for Democracy and Development in Abuja, "There is a general belief that Jonathan hasn't committed himself to fight against Boko Haram because he thought it was a political crusade against him and did not understand that it was a real terrorist movement."[59] He went on to persuade every Nigerian who cared to watch his BBC interview that everything will be alright[60] with this administration since all current problems came

---

58. See Government's "White Paper on the Report of the Federal Government Investigation Panel on the 2011 Election Violence and Disturbances." Some PDP States also had some unrest. See also Ellul, *Violence*, 5–6, "humans can retain control of violence . . . violence can be kept in the service of order and justice and even of peace."

59. Findlay, *Toronto Star*, A8.

60. Plato refers to the "noble lie" which is applicable to our discourse on Ellul's approach to myths and half-truths. See Plato, *The Republic*, Book 111, 389c and Book V, 459c. See also Marlin, *Propaganda and the Ethics of Persuasion*, 146.

from past leaders and the last government, yet Okupe was part of the past (Obasanjo's) government as a spokesman[61], although for a limited time. He continually spins the future of Nigerians by claiming that Nigeria will always get it right in such a way as to showcase what one could refer as the idea of "deified guardians of life."[62] In this case, their analysis portrays President Jonathan and his key cabinet ministers as true *politico-connoisseurs* of a progressive Nigeria. This propaganda approach by media personnel of the government disallows "personal reflection and evaluation" of what the real situation is for the people.[63] It prevents people from taking a critical and constructive evaluation of Nigerian society without being hoodwinked by Aso Rock's propaganda machinery's incredible illusions.[64] We have to recall that Ellul suggests that for propaganda to be really successful or effective it needs to be credible and devoid of illusions. The problem of denial of clear facts and falsification of information to justify the ruling government's perspective is a failure in Jonathan's political transformation agenda and promises. In 2014 alone, there are many incredible political illusions about economic progress in Nigeria. Some of the statistics from government agencies do not add up and the concrete situation reports on economic progress are quite damning.[65] Within such a situation of propaganda and political illusions, David W. Gill explains, "one of the most remarkable insights of Ellul's reflections on propaganda is that propaganda does not just foist lies and falsehoods on its target audiences. It mobilizes its audiences to embrace and act upon accepted 'facts' and the orientation of their mythologies. Propaganda plays on prejudices, it doesn't just create them."[66] Propaganda makes use of prejudice and manipulative style to elicit compliance of the people. From the above one discerns that propaganda involves

61. Bayo Oluwasanmi refers to Doyin Okupe as an insider in Aso Rock Propaganda Empire.

62. See Fowler, *A Synopsis and Analysis of the Thought and Writings of Jacques Ellul.*

63. Ibid.

64. Aso Rock is the seat of governance of the federal republic of Nigeria in Abuja.

65. I am considering at this point the number of young people that died during the Nigerian Immigration Service Recruitment Test stampede in 2014. It is estimated that about 18 young people died. The huge number that participated in that shameful recruitment tests points to the high level of unemployment which has a role in driving the Boko Haram youth into unacceptable alliances with terrorism. This is poverty in action!

66. Gill, "The Word of Jacques Ellul," 23.

social scientific insights and psychological techniques to "sway over human affairs"[67] according to the interest of the propagandist.

As noted earlier, one of the serious cases of terrorism in Nigeria was the kidnap of Chibok Girls. When it happened, the government/ruling party was taken unawares and their initial response was to depict the Opposition parties as bearers of bad news or initiators of protests to set off a false alarm. According to Ifeanyi Izeze, "[A]t the beginning and heat of the *Bring Back Our Girls* protest, the PDP [Peoples Democratic Party] was busy accusing the APC (All Progressives Congress party) of politicizing the abduction of the girls by sponsoring the Oby Ezekwesili-led group, while the opposition in turn also accused the ruling party of coming up with the new group to counter the entire idea."[68] These propaganda activities at some point were pushed too far in order to sway society and the citizenry to the respective sides of the various political parties. It was poorly managed by the government and their communication (propaganda) offices.

Ellul, in the light of the above, thinks that propaganda always has an effect. It does not really fail. What fails is the "surface propaganda, tactical propaganda," but fundamental propaganda succeeds.[69] Propaganda overwhelms us by urging that we stay and wait until answers are given to us instead of finding them out ourselves. We are told what to believe! When to act! What to say! Propaganda is effective through public opinion (the individual participates in public opinion) or "massified" form of opinion.[70]

The Chibok Crisis: The Height

With increased public demand to free the Chibok girls, and the consequent growing criticism of government's lack of leadership, the Nigerian government inaugurated a committee on May 2, 2014 to gather more facts about the kidnapping. Presently, some facts of the Chibok kidnap have been officially disclosed by the Presidential Fact Finding Committee led by Retired Major-General Ibrahim Sabo. The committee states that 276 girls were abducted, 57 escaped, 119 students escaped from the school premises during the abduction. The actual number of missing students is 219.[71] This

67. Kluver, "Jacques Ellul," 101.

68. Izeze, "Bringbackourgirls."

69. Ellul, *Propaganda*, 285.

70. Ibid., p. 291.

71. Umar, "Boko Haram kills 31 people, kills 191."

information is necessary to better understand the issues surrounding the abduction of the girls. If the facts were immediately gathered and authenticated, then it would have shown that government is committed to ensuring security of the people against attacks by Boko Haram and the release of the girls, without orchestrating false information.[72]

The Boko Haram insurgency is clearly a war time situation, at least for millions of Northern Nigerians whose communities have been repeatedly attacked and threatened by the terrorists. Those directly affected are Nigerian citizens whose homes were destroyed and family members were killed, or kidnapped. According to Ellul, "[I]n time of war, everybody agrees that news must be limited and controlled,"[73] but in Nigeria's case it shows a colossal failure of propaganda and failure to communicate with the people by government. The situation is what Prof. Abiodun Salawu, Professor of Journalism, Communication and Media Studies, North-West University, South Africa, describes that the presidency urgently needs a proactive and convincing information office. Now let us take a brief look at Boko Haram itself.

The Boko Haram crisis in Nigeria has bedeviled the country for over five years now. The devastations are enormous and undeniable. It has already dragged the economy and lives of Northeastern Nigeria to a terrible halt. Some of these people are internally displaced persons (IDP)[74] and some are refugees in other countries sharing boundaries with that part of Nigeria. A *Toronto Star* newspaper report by Haruna Umar and Michelle Faul provides updates on the level of devastation after the eight months following the kidnap of the 219 Chibok girls. The current report affirms that, "[I]n a recent video, Shekau said the girls were "an old story," implying their release was no longer up for negotiation."[75] Of course, Boko Haram's leader in Nigeria—Mr. Shekau—was reported killed many months ago by the

---

72. The recent terrorist attack in Paris where 12 people were killed showed the preparedness of government in addressing the issues, getting at the three terrorists, and apologizing for failing to forestall the attack in spite of earlier intelligence reports. The incident was followed by a march of world leaders and the people of France, about one million strong, declaring: "Je suis Charlie," meaning "I am Charlie." The important point here is to avoid distortion or manipulation of facts. It demands giving the people the facts of the situation and in a good time.

73. Ellul, *Propaganda*, 238. See also Ellul, *Violence*.

74. There are about 4 million internally displaced persons in Nigeria. About 1.5 million persons were displaced by the Boko Haram menace.

75. Umar, "Boko Haram."

Nigerian military, even with purported pictures as evidence of his corpse. With this level of miscommunication and non-convincing approach to the use of propaganda, we now consider the impact of failed propaganda.

The situation of Boko Haram terrorism has caused some eminent Nigerians to express dissatisfaction with the failure of leadership and ineffective communication relationship between the government and the Nigerian people. The former president of Nigeria, retired General Olusegun Obasanjo—an experienced leader and officer in his own right—has tried to weigh into the situation, and offer some critical assistance.

Propaganda and Ex-President Obasanjo

Former President Obasanjo is of the view that Jonathan's leadership has isolated many prominent Nigerians who could have been useful in addressing the current security and unemployment problems. Obasanjo's first criticism against the Nigerian government war against terrorism is the inability of government to accept well-tested and credible authorities to assist in the war against Boko Haram, and to help mediate in the release of the kidnapped Chibok Girls' case. Jonathan's government, according to him, has, in principle, aligned itself with some bad elements and corrupt politicians while excluding resourceful prominent ex-leaders who may not agree with Jonathan's unpopular policies and security approaches. These accusations and other critical comments from Obasanjo were countered with firm propaganda by the spokesmen of the president. Ellul, in line with this situation, states that "[P]ropaganda is by itself a state of war; it demands the exclusion of opposite trends and minorities—not total and official perhaps, but . . . partial and indirect exclusion."[76] Propaganda is not only meant to elicit cooperation from citizens, but also crush the ability (of citizens) to shape their lives and their understanding of events.

In December 2014, Obasanjo said he wrote a letter to President Jonathan, entitled "Before It Is Too Late." In the letter he advised Jonathan to "[M]ove away from culture of denials, cover-ups and proxies and deal honesty, sincerely and transparently with Nigerians to regain their trust and confidence." He adds, "Nigerians are no fools, they can see, they can hear, they can talk among themselves, they can think, they can compare and they can act in the interest of their country and in their own self-interest. They keenly watch all actions and deeds that are associated with you if they

76. Ellul, *Propaganda*, 247.

cannot believe your words. I know you have the power to save PDP[Peoples' Democratic Party] and the country. I beg you to have the courage and the will with patriotism to use the power for the good of the country."[77] He also requested that the current opportunity will serve to right the many wrongs of the current president and reassure Nigerians in the face of terrorism.

As is a well-known, senior citizens and eminent political figures sometimes consider certain duties to their fatherland/motherland as an *opportune* call to duty—a duty of conscience! [78] They may feel the need to offer a timeless political service for the common good of their people and to offer generous services to their nations in appreciation for what they have received in terms of honor and respect. In this light, Ellul rightly notes, "nothing is worse in times of danger than to live in a dream world. To warn a political system of a menace hanging over it does not imply an attack against it, but the greatest service one can render the system."[79]

The failure to accept the assistance of eminent Nigerians and other responsible authorities in prosecuting the war against terrorism by President Jonathan has left him with damning criticisms from international observers and commentators. For instance, Gwynne Dyer expressed the incompetence of the current leadership in Nigeria, especially in its inability to prosecute the war against terrorism/Boko Haram.[80] Prof. Pius Adesanmi described the whole situation of manipulative communication by spokespersons of government with a catch phrase as "career Jonathanism."[81] 'Career Jonathanism' refers to the effort of people working for the Nigerian government to manipulate, clean-up, defend, rationalise, and wipe-out any dent of poor publicity by the current president. But one has to note that Ellul is not really after perfect accomplishments, but he demands a humane communication of the facts that will bring about peace and development in the society. It is on this note that we take a look at the failure of propaganda in Nigeria, especially in light of President Jonathan's spokesperson—Dr. Okupe.

77. Saharareporters, "President Jonathan."

78. Anozie, "The Duty to Help and Duty to Responsible Justice."

79. Ellul, *Propaganda*, xvi.

80. Dyer, "Boko Haram not Nigeria's only Problem," A4. Gwynne Dyer is an independent journalist based in London, England.

81 Saharareporters, "President Jonathan."

Failure of Propaganda: Okupe's Ostrich Experience

Jonathan's government and spokespersons are of the view that Boko Haram is an instrument of the main Opposition party and of some Northern elements who feel they do not control government and thus use terrorism as the best way to get the attention of government.[82] It seems to tally with what Ellul describes (he agrees with Marx) as, "when man realizes that he no longer has the means of influencing the situation he begins to revolt."[83] But one is not sure of the credibility of such insinuations against the Opposition parties and some Northern elites. The main Opposition party members are Nigerians whose contributions to governance must be considered and incorporated, without being badmouthed through dirty propaganda and divisive publications. It is the duty of those in government to show quality leadership in communicating with dignity and humanly for a peaceful society. This is what it means to have an inclusive democracy and governance without playing dirty game or distorting information to win political gains.

With the primaries[84] of the various political parties in Nigeria now over, a good number of the ministers in Jonathan's government failed to make it in the primaries of their PDP party. This could be an indication of the failure of propaganda, especially in the case of former minister Maku, who was once a vivacious Minister of Information. He traveled all over Nigeria convincing people of the accomplishments of Jonathan's administration and suppressing some of Jonathan's leadership weaknesses. SaharaReporters states, "[T]he seven ministers, who resigned on October 15 [2014] included Information Minister, Labaran Maku, Health Minister, Professor Onyebuchi Chukwu and Nyesom Wike, Minister of State for Education. Others were Samuel Ortom, Minister of State for Industry, Trade and Investment; Musiliu Obanikoro, Minister of State for Defence; Darius Ishaku, Minister of State for Niger Delta and Chief Emeka Wogu, Minister of Labour and Productivity."[85] We could also look at other significant ministries once occupied by some of the ministers belonging to the ruling government PDP. Even a minister of health during the successful

---

82. Some elder statesmen like Chief Edwin Clark (Ijaw Chief) have shared this opinion too about Boko Haram and the Opposition parties.

83. Ellul, *Jacques Ellul on Politics, Technology and Christianity*, 24.

84. Primaries are election procedures for a political party to nominate her best candidates for the multi-party level campaign before elections. They could be related to US party conventions to select promising candidates to represent the party.

85. Saharareporters, "President Jonathan."

effort against Ebola Disease in Nigeria, Prof. Onyebuchi Chukwu, failed to be elected in his PDP party primaries.[86]

As Ellul states in this case "[T]he individual perceives only that propaganda that his personality lets him perceive, but his personality is changed by that propaganda."[87] Propaganda surely affects the propagandist like a fellow who is no longer seeing life as the reality. Our duty to society, according to Ellul, is to be aware of the conditions of reality, the conditions of our world. He calls it "the duty of understanding the world and oneself."[88] It is a duty also to disclose these effects of propaganda on propagandists and the people/society.

One of the effects of propaganda is to sell the myth of success and well-being or of progress. Marlin presents this Ellulian perspective in these words, "[T]hese myths, of progress, happiness, work, race, the hero, and suchlike, operate on a broader spectrum than merely the political, but they can also diminish human freedom."[89] The events in Nigeria are situations that people are interested in because their lives and their families are affected. We are dealing with terrorism and loss of human life, not mere calculation covered up through propaganda.[90]

With Boko Haram hell bent on such a barbaric terrorist mission, Nigeria truly needs a disciplined leader with clear incorruptible qualities. That leader also needs the communicative skills and qualities that Ellul describes to be able to rally the people in a situation of war. Whether President Jonathan will revive these desirable potential he may possess to still be the president, or whether the incorruptible qualities needed to overcome Boko Haram are present in Retired Brigadier General Buhari to lead Nigeria, that is for history to record as from May 2015, if the elections hold. Ellul envisions that we all need the ethics of communicating humanly to maintain a peaceful world and overcome terrorism. Any party that wins the forth-coming election will still need the collaboration of other parties to keep Nigeria's nascent democracy and maintain a common front that supports the values of intelligible/credible democracy. We surely need a

86. Ebola containment was a great success in APC controlled states, such as Lagos and the Rivers States. With such a political divide is it right to attribute such success to President Jonathan?

87. Ellul, *Propaganda*, 264.

88. Greenman, *Understanding Jacques Ellul*, 17.

89. Marlin, "Problems in Ellul's Treatment of Propaganda," 9.

90. Prof. Cornel West refers to Obama's effort on racism in America as guided by political calculation rather than by morality or conviction.

government that will, through Ellul's insightful perspective, eliminate any form of "dehumanize [ing] experience[s] . . . [that] undermine democracy and critical intelligence."[91]

Conclusion

Ellul desires a total approach to the critical problems of humanity. He talks about terrorism, propaganda and politics all having a role to play in human total liberation, dignity, and enjoyment of the common good. As he says, it is about understanding humanity, community and our history.[92] The duty of the Nigerian government is to look at life from this same holistic perspective. That is, to address the real issues that likely will enhance the little success stories about Nigeria's nascent democracy.

Nigeria as a democratic state needs more than mere political sophistry and rhetoric, mere political action and propaganda to change the onslaught of terrorism sustained by corruption and unemployment. As Ellul notes, society is never better off when we rely merely on "political action" and propaganda. So far, Boko Haram is after Nigeria's disintegration, but government needs to work with the Opposition parties in a way to showcase a strong, vibrant, and united front. The same applies to the media spokespeople of the Presidency. They must communicate in a way that does not mislead the people, denigrate the supporters of the Opposition parties in collaboratively building a cohesive Nigeria capable of tackling terrorism and corruption. Corruption and terrorism and unemployment are Nigeria's state-of-emergency problems! All Nigerian citizens, including representatives of government, and members of the Opposition parties ought to focus on the facts without distortions, stand for mutual respect and peace, and defend the survival of our emerging democracy.

References

Anozie, Stanley. "The Duty to Help and Duty to Responsible Justice in light of Alan Gewirth's The Community of Rights." Paper delivered at the *Alternative Perspective and Global Concerns International Conference*. University of Ottawa, October 17–18, 2014.

91. Kluver, "Jacques Ellul," 99.
92. Greenman, *Understanding Jacques Ellul*, 4.

———. "Human Rights and Terrorism: The Niger Delta Oil War." In *Morality and Terrorism: an Interfaith Perspective*, edited by Mahmoud Masaeli, 206–25. Orange County, CA: Nortia, 2012.

Audu, Sunday D. "The Almajiri Institution, Boko Haram, and Terrorism in Northern Nigeria." In *Morality and Terrorism: an Interfaith Perspective*, edited by Mahmoud Masaeli, 184–94. Orange County, California: Nortia, 2012.

Doki "Chibok: Terrorism's New Face" *Vanguard*, June 9, 2014. Online: http://www.vanguardngr.com/2014/06/chibok-terrorisms-new-face/.

Dyer, Gwynne. "Boko Haram not Nigeria's only problem." *The Peterborough Examiner*, Thursday, December 4, 2014.

Ellul, Jacques. "The Ethics of Propaganda." *Communication*. 6 (1981) 159–75. Translated by D. Raymond Tourville. http://ellul.org/ELLUL%20FORUM%20ARTICLES/ISSUE37.pdf.

———. *The Humiliation of the Word*. Translated by Joyce Main Hanks. Grand Rapids: Eerdmans, 1985.

———. *Propaganda: The Formation of Men's Attitudes*. Translated by Konrad Kellen and Jean Lerner. New York: Vintage, 1965.

———. *The Technological Bluff*. Translated by Geoffrey W. Bromiley. Grand Rapids: Eerdmans, 1990.

———. *Violence; Reflections from a Christian Perspective*. Translated by Cecelia Gaul Kings. New York: Seabury, 1969.

Ellul, Jacques, and Patrick Troude-Chastenet. *Jacques Ellul on Politics, Technology, and Christianity*. Translated by Joan Mendes-France. Eugene, OR: Wipf & Stock, 2005.

Findlay, Stephanie. "Weary Voters Look to Former Military Leader." *Toronto Star*, Friday, January 30, 2015.

Fowler, James A. "A Synopsis and Analysis of the Thought and Writings of Jacques Ellul." www.christinyou.com/pages/ellul.html.

Halton, David. *Dispatches from the Front: Matthew Halton, Canada's Voice at War*. Toronto: McClelland & Stewart, 2014.

Gill, David W. "The Word of Jacques Ellul." *Ellul Forum* 37 (2006) 23–24.

Glander, Timothy Richard. *Origins of Mass Communications Research During the American Cold War*. London: Routledge, 2000.

Greenman, Jeffrey, P., et al. *Understanding Jacques Ellul*. Eugene, OR: Wipf and Stock, 2013.

Ifeanyi Izeze, "#Bringbackourgirls: Tragedy of A Divided Nigerian People." http://saharareporters.com/article/bringbackourgirls-tragedy-divided-nigerian-people-ifeanyi-izeze.

Konyndyk, Kenneth J. "Violence." In *Jacques Ellul: Interpretive Essays*, edited by Clifford G. Christians & Jay M. Van Hook, 251–69. Chicago: University of Illinois Press, 1981.

Kluver, Randy. "Jacques Ellul: Technique, Propaganda, and Modern Media." In *Perspectives on Culture, Technology and Communication: The Media Ecology Tradition*, edited by Casey Lum, 97–116. Cresskill, NJ: Hampton Press, 2006.

Lasswell, Harold, D. and Dorothy Blumenstock. *World Revolutionary Propaganda*. New York: Alfred A. Knopf, 1939.

Marlin, Randall. "Problems in Ellul's Treatment of Propaganda." *Ellul Forum* 37 (2006) 9–12.

———. *Propaganda & the Ethics of Persuasion*. Ontario, Canada: Broadview, 2002.

Minteh, Binneh and Ashlie Perry. *Terrorism in West Africa—Boko Haram's Evolution, Strategy and Affiliations,* presented at the Mid-West Political Science Association's 71st Annual Conference, Chicago, April, 2013. http://papers.ssrn.com/sol3/papers.cfm?abstract_id=2313906.

Nasr, Seyyed Hossein. *Islam: Religion, History, and Civilization.* New York: HarperCollins, 2003.

Okolo, Chukwudum, C. *Squandermania Mentality: Reflections on Nigerian Culture.* Enugu, Nigeria: University Trust, 1994.

Oyebade, Adebayo. "Reluctant Democracy: The State, the Opposition, and the Crisis of Political Transition, 1985–1993." In *The Transformation of Nigeria: Essays in Honor of Toyin Falola,* edited by Adebayo Oyebade, 137–67. Trenton, NJ: Africa World, 2002.

Plato. *The Collected Dialogues of Plato.* Edited by Edith Hamilton and Huntington Cairns. Translated by W. D. Woodhead. New York: Pantheon, 1961.

Saharareporters. "President Jonathan Sends Frontline PDP Governors to Beg Most Prominent Critic, Obasanjo." *SAHA,* December 2, 2014. http://saharareporters.com/2014/12/04/president-jonathan-sends-frontline-pdp-governors-beg-most-prominent-critic-obasanjo.

Umar, Haruna and Michelle Faul. "Boko Haram kills 31 people, kills 191." *Toronto Star,* December 19, 2014. Online: http://www.thestar.com/news/world/2014/12/18/boko_haram_kills_31_people_kidnaps_191.html.

Doki "Chibok: Terrorism's new face" *Vanguard,* June 9 2014. http://www.vanguardngr.com/2014/06/chibok-terrorisms-new-face/.

Chapter 7

Ellul, Machiavelli, and Autonomous Technique[1]

Richard Kirkpatrick

"In spite of the frequent mention of Machiavelli's *Prince*, the truth is that until the beginning of the twentieth century no one ever drew the technical consequences of that work."[2] Jacques Ellul thus remarks without elaboration in *The Technological Society*, although he had more elsewhere to say about Niccolò Machiavelli (1469–1527), as appears below. While many have noted a "technical" dimension to Machiavelli's thought,[3] none

---

1. My thanks to Professors David Lovekin and Jeffrey Shaw for help shaping this paper.

2. Ellul, *Technological Society,* 232.

3. An early twentieth-century example, perhaps one Ellul had in mind, was Schmitt, *Dictatorship*, 6–7, cited in McCormick, *Carl Schmitt's Critique of Liberalism*, 129–30 (finding in Machiavelli "purely technical interests . . . technicity"). Ruffo-Fiore, in *Niccolo Machiavelli*, collects many articles and books touching on Machiavelli's "technical" approach and "technique." Some interpreters of Machiavelli have equated or conflated the terms "technical" and "scientific" (e.g., Hughes in "The Science of Machiavelli"). Also see Cassirer, *The Myth of the State,* 153, under the caption "The Technique of Politics," for a comparison of Machiavelli with Galileo. The interpretation of "Machiavelli the Scientist," which flowered mid-twentieth century (see Singleton, "The Perspective of Art"), was widely criticized. Moravia, "Machiavelli," 128, in a penetrating essay distinguishes Machiavelli the technician and Machiavelli the scientist, as, apparently, does Strauss; compare *Thoughts on Machiavelli,* 20 and "Three Waves of Modernity," 86–87. In nuanced passages, Ellul considered "science" and "technique" to be related, but he regarded technique as a separate phenomenon, and, in its modern stages of extreme acceleration,

has considered it specifically in light of Ellul's conception of "autonomous technique"—deterministic technique that is "self-directing." Ellul's main study was the "technical system" as a civilizational phenomenon, the historical origins of which he found in the eighteenth century CE.[4] Thus, Machiavelli—two hundred years before then—was unquestionably far from the fully realized "technical system" in its modern maturity, and extreme contemporary acceleration. Ellul, however, glimpsed in his thought early characteristics or symptoms of the phenomenon of technique applied to humans—"a lightning flash," as one scholar put it, "long before the main storm."[5] This chapter presents Machiavelli's pertinent line of thought and brief extracts from the *Prince*, the *Discourses*, and his letters,[6] then draws the technical consequences in Ellul's terms

Niccolò Machiavelli

"On many occasions," Machiavelli wrote,[7] he considered a dilemma, in sum: You consistently do your will and reach your intended ends when you adapt yourself and match your "modes of proceeding" (*modi del procedere*)[8] to changes of fortune and of the times. Everyone, however, has a given nature, so you are *unable* adapt as needed. Fortune and the times change, but you, stuck in your nature, do not—to your ruin. When Machiavelli counsels you "to use" the lion and to use the fox,[9] he knows it impossible—the fox is no more leonine than the lion is vulpine; the same

---

to have precedence over science. My observations on Machiavelli in this piece are strictly limited to the terms of Ellul's conception of "autonomous technique."

4. Ellul, *Technological System*, 79 and Ellul, *Perspectives on Our Age*, 29–30.

5. Cranz, *Technology and Western Reason*, 24.

6. Citation to the *Prince* are by chapter numbers, and to the *Discourses* by Book and chapter numbers, which are standard in all editions.

7. Bondanella, *Niccolò Machiavelli, Discourses on Livy*, 281 (*Discourses* 3.9: "Io ho considerato più volte . . . "). See also Ridolfi, "*I Ghiribizzi al Soderini*," 53, a critical edition of the text at Martelli, Machiavelli *Opere*, 1082 - 83; see also the tercets on Fortuna at *Opere*, 978 lines 103–05, 112, 112, 114, 126; Inglese, *Machiavelli Capitoli*, 122–23; McCanles, *The Discourse of Il Principe*, Chapter 25; *Opere*, 1136–39, 1252–56 (April 29, 1513 letter to Vettori); *Opere*, 295–96 (*Prince* 25); 211–14 (*Discourses* 3.8—9); 226–27 (*Discourses* 3.21); 956 (*L'Asino*).

8. As translated by Mansfield in *Machiavelli: Discourses on Livy* and *Machiavelli: The Prince*.

9. For the composite man-beast, the centaur, see Raimondi, "The Centaur and the Politician," in Ascoli & Kahn, *Machiavelli and the Discourse of Literature*, 145–60.

inflexibility is to be found in humans, whose stubborn natures obstruct their wills.[10] We get in the way of our own goals.

In this as in all his observations and reading, Machiavelli presents examples of "the actions of great men."[11] Two of his favorite ancient exemplars of modes of proceeding were Hannibal the Carthaginian and Scipio the Roman—opposites: Scipio used the mode of "love" with "piety, fidelity, and religion," Hannibal, the mode of fear, with "cruelty, perfidy and irreligion."[12] Both were successful, but, changing times and fortunes might have required reversal: Hannibal to adopt the mode of love, and Scipio, fear, or yet other modes. These men, however, being unable to adapt themselves and their modes, would have failed. As Professor Ferroni summarizes:

> The guarantee of happiness and success can be offered, in Machia-velli's anthropology, only by the individual's capacity for adapting his particular nature to the variations of Fortune, and thus of repeatedly "transforming" the modes of proceeding, according to the directions of these variations. If Fortune moves continuously between extreme and opposite poles, we will be able to match her only if we also know equally well how to shuttle between extremes, only if we are always ready to reverse our own mode of proceeding (if, in sum, we succeed in "transforming into the contrary").[13]

One of Machiavelli's well-known attempted answers to the problem is *virtù*,[14] a force of nature to match capricious Fortuna, by "beating her and holding her down."[15] *Virtù* is a personal gift—ancient, atavistic and, as Machiavelli knows, rarely to be found. *Virtù* is extraordinary, personal, natural—the "modes of proceeding" are abstract, universal, impersonal. "Modes" do not much matter to those having "great *virtù*" or "extraordinary *virtù*"[16], but few have *virtù* at all, and fewer still have it in abundance. "The operations of greatest *virtù*" are things of the past.[17] If *virtù* is not in your

10. Greenwood, "Machiavelli and the Problem of Human Inflexibility," 196.

11. The quoted passage is from Machiavelli's dedication of the *Prince*.

12. Ridolfi, "*I Ghiribizzi al Soderini*," note 6. Book III Chapter 21 of the Discourses is titled "Whence It Arises that with a Different Mode of Proceeding Hannibal Produced Those Same Effects in Italy as Scipio Did in Spain." *Discourses* 3.21.

13. Ferroni. "Transformation," 19.

14. For a start on the enormous bibliography of *virtù*, see Mansfield, *Machiavelli: Discourses on Livy*, 315–16.

15. *Prince*, 25.

16. *Discourses*, 3.21.

17. *Discourses*, Preface to Book 1.

given nature, you cannot hope to acquire it. Besides, a savage who possesses *virtù* may flex it without consulting Machiavelli. *Virtù*, the natural force, does not answer Machiavelli's procedural problem—to find modes accessible to those who understand (*intende*) and who "know" fortune and the times,[18] so that they always (*sempre*) reach their ends successfully.[19]

Another of Machiavelli's responses to the problem is pretense, but only to disguise personal qualities in yourself you cannot change or to simulate qualities you do not have. As to morals, you need not "have them in fact" but only "appear to have them," and it may be advantageous sometimes even "to be" so. "But the mind must be framed in a way that, needing not to be, you can know how to change to the contrary."[20] When, as here, *seeming* and *being* elide, the old dilemma recurs.

As Professor Najemy explains:

> Particularly thorny for Machiavelli was the philosophical conundrum of agency and contingency. . . . The unpredictability of events, the irrationality of history, and people's inability to deviate from their inborn nature and inclinations (all of which flow into what he meant by fortune) caused him to wonder where and how agency, or free will, could determine or influence the outcome of events (which is at least one important sense of Machiavellian *virtù*). . . . If, in theory, random variation and unpredictability can be tamed either by prudence or impetuosity, in practice *both methods are rendered inefficacious by the prison of unchanging individual natures that occludes the required flexibility.* In his poetry and letters Machiavelli recast the problem by relocating the "variation" of fortune in both nature and human nature, and thus no longer only in external randomness. . . . [T]his theoretical dilemma . . . never ceased to trouble him.[21]

Machiavelli scholar Professor Atkinson adds: "The question would continue to haunt him. . . ."[22]

Culminating his long search for accessible and consistently effective modes of proceeding, Machiavelli was led in a radically new

18. Ridolfi, "*I Ghiribizzi al Soderini*," note 6. "Et veramente chi fussi tanto *savio* che *conoscessi* e tempi e l'ordine delle cose et adcomodassisi ad quelle . . . ." Martelli, Machiavelli Opere 1083a (emphasis added).

19. *Prince*, 15; *Discourses* 3.21.

20. *Prince*, 18.

21. Najemy, *Cambridge Companion to Machiavelli*, 11 (emphasis added).

22. Atkinson, *Niccolo Machiavelli: A Portrait*, 18–19.

direction—"dans d'étranges domaines," as Ellul calls the realm of the technical bluff.[23] In Machiavelli's letter dated April 29, 1513, the main subject is the latest in political news, the truce between the king of France and Ferdinand, king of Spain. Machiavelli exhaustively argues both sides of the case—that Ferdinand was wise in his modes, then, with equal facility, the reverse: that he was unwise. Machiavelli ventures a third alternative:

> One of the modes (*modi*) for holding on to new territories and for either stabilizing equivocal *minds* or keeping them hanging and irresolute is to arouse great expectations of oneself, always keeping men's *minds* busy with trying to figure out the end (*fine*) of one's decisions and one's new ventures. The king has recognized the need for this and has employed it to advantage . . . He has not tried to foresee the end (*fine*): for his end (*fine*) is not so much this, that, or the other victory, as to win prestige among his various peoples and to keep them hanging with his multifarious activities. Therefore he has always been a spirited maker of beginnings, later giving them that end (*fine*) which chance places before him or which necessity teaches him.[24]

The reader may well wonder if the theory makes "any coherent sense" and consider it, as Machiavelli himself allowed, a stingray "sold with its tail lopped off," that is, a "fish without head or tail"—in vernacular, "without rhyme or reason"[25] — "higgledy-piggledy."[26] We have, however, two versions of the letter, one draft, one final; the great epistolographer says what he wishes, how he wishes.

Ferdinand reappears as an exemplar in the *Prince*, in which Machiavelli promises to deliver the "effectual truth" (*verità effettuale*).[27] By attacking Granada, Machiavelli writes, Ferdinand

> kept the minds of the barons of Castile preoccupied; while thinking of that war, they did not think of [political] innovations.[28] By this means (*mezzo*), without their realizing it, he acquired great prestige and authority over them . . . Thus he consistently planned and executed great projects which have always kept the minds of

23. Ellul, *Technological Bluff*, xvi.

24. Atkinson & Sices, *The Sweetness of Power*, 235 (emphasis added).

25. Najemy, *Between Friends*, 126.

26. Atkinson & Sices, *Machiavelli and His Friends*, 236, 506.

27. *Prince*, 15.

28. Rinaldi, *Machiavelli, Opere, Volume 1 Tome 1*, 345 note 17, explains the political connotations of "*innovazione*."

his subjects in suspense and wonder—concentrated on the out-
come (*evento*) of events. His moves have followed so closely one
upon the other that he has never given men an ample enough interval between his exploits to work quietly against him.[29]

A hypothetical figure comparable to Ferdinand appears in Machiavelli's *Discourses*. Machiavelli notes that "men are desirous of new things."[30]

This desire, therefore, opens the doors to anyone in a province
who makes himself the leader of an innovation: if he is a foreigner,
they run after him; if he is from the province, they gather around
him, augmenting and favoring him so that however he proceeds
he succeeds in making great strides in those places.[31]

This "Innovator" may be a reformer, seditionist, or busy politician. His in-
novations are much like Ferdinand's "beginnings" and "great enterprises."
Ferdinand makes up his nominal "ends" as he goes along; Machiavelli's Innovator has no identified ends at all. He has no name. Machiavelli gives
no exemplar among men past or present. In neither the Innovator nor
Ferdinand does Machiavelli identify *virtù*; they do not need it. Nor do they
need to dissemble to succeed. Constant action itself blinds people, or, as
spectacle, fascinates them. The success, "needing not to be" anybody, is,
literally—nobody. In sum, this idea is a perfect example of "autonomous
technique" in the thought of Jacques Ellul.

Jacques Ellul

Ellul's conception of "autonomous technique" illuminates Machiavelli's
novel thoughts on Ferdinand and the Innovator. Technique becomes autonomous, Ellul explains, when one "method (*méthode*) is manifestly the
most efficient (*plus efficiente*) of all the other means (*moyens*)," —at that
crux— "the technical movement becomes self-directing. . . . The human
being is no longer in any sense the agent of choice. . . . He does not make
a choice of complex, and, in some way, human motives. He can decide
only in favor of the technique that gives maximum efficiency (*le maximum*

---

29. *Prince*, 21 (emphasis added).

30. *Discourses*, 3.21: "gli uomini sono desiderosi di cose nuove." (Martelli, Machiavelli Opere 227a); *Discourses* 1.37: "gli uomini sogliono affliggersi nel male e stuccarsi
nel bene" (Id, 119a).

31. *Discourses*, 3.21.

d'efficience)."[32] Autonomous technique "is an end in itself. . . . Technique obeys its own determinations, it realizes itself (*elle se réalize elle-même*)."[33]

Ellul teaches that, from "the moment efficacy (*l'efficacité*) becomes the criterion of political action" no one can choose (*ne pourrait choisir*) by any other criterion. Ellul writes that Machiavelli "does in fact conclude that politics is autonomous. Doctrine enters only when he tries to establish general rules (*une politique générale*) and formulate the political courses that he considers the most efficient, having first established efficiency as a value. . . . Machiavelli really demonstrated the Prince's role, above all, is to be effective (*efficace*). By doing so, he introduced a new perspective, revolutionized his time, introduced efficiency (*l'efficacité*) as a value."[34]

When discussing Machiavelli's "theory of prestige and of diversion," Ellul cites the passage of the *Prince*, quoted above, on Ferdinand, and adds:

> The prince must first ensure his prestige by psychological means, and secondly he must divert the attention of his opponents and of his subjects on questions that impassion them while he himself acts in another domain. . . . Although Machiavelli did not devote a special chapter to propaganda, one can say that it is everywhere in his work, that he is the premier theoretician of propaganda (*le premier théoricien de la propaganda*), and that his theory is famously encapsulated: "to govern is to make believe (*gouverner, c'est faire croire*)."[35]

After a long, frustrating effort to mediate possibility and necessity, ends and means, Machiavelli's "philosophical conundrum" is not solved, but erased. Machiavelli's Ferdinand and Innovator are entrained in modes of proceeding that are autonomous, self-directing. Ferdinand circles endlessly:

- His means are to keep people guessing about his end, so

- He takes actions without seeing their end, because

- His end is to keep people guessing.

32. Ellul, *Technological Society*, 80 ("les autres moyens" appears in the original French).

33. Ellul, *Technological System*, 125, 141. See also Ellul, *Technological Bluff*, 243.

34. Ellul, *Political Illusion*, 69–70.

35. Ellul, *Histoire de la Propagande*, 47–48.

The stingray with its tail lopped off is circular, and circles have no "end."[36] Ferdinand undertakes ceaseless actions without seeing their ends as the means to hold people in "suspense and wonder" about his ends; nobody can make "heads or tails" of him. Ferdinand's "ends" are whatever happens. In the *Discourses*, the Innovator has no stated ends whatsoever; he does nothing but innovate—*what* is unspecified. "However he proceeds he succeeds"—*to what purpose* is unspecified. He fascinates people—*why* is unspecified. Spectacle and fascination are technically related,[37] and both support Ferdinand's dominion of everyone's minds.

For both Ferdinand's "great enterprises" and the Innovator's "great strides," unnamed ends have disappeared into technique, which is its own end. To adapt Ellul, Ferdinand and the Innovator have set out "at tremendous speed—to go *nowhere* (*vers nulle part*)."[38] Machiavelli's technical "modes" in the political world are what Ellul calls "make believe" or "*Le Bluff Technologique*."[39] Ellul scholar Professor David Lovekin explains that Ellul's technique "is always artificial . . . and abstractive."[40] Machiavelli anticipates our own technically abstract vocabulary as applied to humans: modes, procedures, operations,[41] managing.[42]

The solution to the means-ends problem that so vexed Machiavelli, in the revolutionary terms of autonomous technique, is technically "sweet." For Ferdinand and the Innovator, the "effectual truth" (Machiavelli) and the "means absolutely most efficient" (Ellul) have no ends. Says Ellul: "the ends have disappeared, or they seem to have no connection with means . . . The means no longer have any need of the end . . . [Technique] goes where every step leads it, an implacable monster which nothing can stop."[43] Paradoxically, Machiavelli intended the modes of proceeding as a way to preserve

36. Montanari, *La Poesia del Machiavelli*, 70 ("circolo della necessità . . . la legge fondamentale della tecnica").

37. Ellul, *Technological Bluff*, xvi, 323ff. See also Ellul, *Humiliation of the Word*, for a discourse on the primacy of spectacle in the technical system.

38. Ellul, *Presence of the Kingdom*, 56 (emphasis in the translation).

39. Ellul, *Technological Bluff*, xvi.

40. Lovekin, *Technique, Discourse, and Consciousness*, 160. See also, Chiapelli, *Studi sul Linguaggio del Machiavelli*, 45–46 for an explanation of the comparably abstract character of Machiavelli's prose.

41. *Discourses*, 1 Preface; the Ghiribizzi of 1506, supra n 5.

42. *Prince*, 9; *Discourses*, 3.40.

43. Ellul, *Presence of the Kingdom*, 54, 59, 60.

"our free will"[44] (*el nostro libero arbitrio*),[45] but autonomous technique is deterministic: Ellul's technical man (*l'homme technicien*) is "absolutely no longer an agent of choice (*n'est absolument plus l'agent du choix*)."

If the technical solution seems irrational—autonomous technique inverts reason and creates a rationality of its own, which Ellul names "unreason." As he explains: "The desire . . . to rationalize human behavior will *always* lead to a point of reversal and an explosion of the irrational. . . . We have here a kind of monster. Each piece is rational but the whole and its functioning are masterpieces of irrationality. . . . There is a process which leads on from apparently sane and acceptable premises to irrational conduct and plans."[46]

In Ferdinand and the Innovator, the apparent absurdity and irrationality of Machiavelli's modes of proceeding are irrelevant to technique, which, for Ellul, is "the triumph of the absurd," culminating in "ultimate idiocies (*ultimes sottises*)."[47] Just as autonomous technique subverts free will, the engine of Machiavelli's modes, it also subverts reason, one of the few standards usually observed by the otherwise infamously subversive Machiavelli.[48] To adapt Benedetto Croce's famous observation by substituting "technique" for "politics:" "Machiavelli discovers the necessity and autonomy of *technique*, of *technique* that is beyond, or, rather, below, moral good and evil, that has its own laws against which it is useless to rebel."[49]

Ellul explains that "the system presupposes a more and more thorough interrogation of each element, including man, as an object . . . a manageable

44. *Prince*, 25.

45. For the crucial importance of the will in Machiavelli, see Singleton, "The Perspectives of Art," 176.

46. Ellul, *Technological Bluff*, 108, 169, 221 (emphasis in the original).

47. Ibid., 197, 381.

48. While variations on *ragione* in Italian have a number of different connotations, Machiavelli's uses emphatically include *ragione*'s noetic sense. See the glossaries in Mansfield, *Machiavelli, The Prince*, 134 and Mansfield, *Machiavelli: Discourses on Livy*, 339–40. See also April 29, 1513, letter, supra n 6: "I do not want to be prompted by any authority but reason (*ragione*)," and, from Mansfield, *Machiavelli: Discourses on Livy*, 1.58: "I do not and I never shall judge the defense of any opinion by reasons (*ragioni*) without recourse to either authority or force to be a flaw." Atkinson and Sices, *Machiavelli and His Friends*, 233.

49. Croce, *Politics and Morals*, 59. "Machiavelli scopre la necessità e l'autonomia della politica, della politica che è di là, o piuttosto di qua, dal bene e dal male morale, che ha le sue leggi a cui è vano ribellarsi." The essay *"Machiavelli e Vico"* was first published in 1924.

object (*d'objet maniable*) . . . in this inhuman universe (*univers inhumain*). . . . Modern man, having been dehumanized by means, [has] himself become a means."[50] Ellul approvingly quotes a commentator: "Technique has nothing to do with inner life except to abolish it (*l'abolir*)."[51]

Scholars have observed the phenomenon in Machiavelli's actors, subjects and objects. They are "raw material."[52] "Have not all readers of Machiavelli felt how his heroes have no inside?" "The image is all, the reality nothing." The prince "must make himself a person with no qualities whatsoever . . . a cipher, possessing no qualities, either bestial or human, as his own. . . . The prince never *is* this or that, he *uses* this or that quality . . . A void at the center of the *Prince* marks the absence of the prince himself." Humans are, in a word, "zero."[53] These are "the technical consequences," in Ellul's terms, to be drawn from Machiavelli's *Prince*.

References

Ascoli, Albert & Victoria Kahn. *Machiavelli and the Discourse of Literature*. Ithaca, NY: Cornell University Press, 1993.

Atkinson, James B. "Niccolò Machiavelli: a Portrait." In *The Cambridge Companion to Machiavelli,* edited by John M. Najemy, 1–13. Cambridge, UK: Cambridge University Press, 2010.

Atkinson, James B. & David Sices. *Machiavelli and His Friends: Their Personal Correspondence*. DeKalb, IL: Northern Illinois University Press, 1996.

———. *The Sweetness of Power: Machiavelli's Discourses & Guicciardini's Considerations*. DeKalb, IL: Northern Illinois University Press, 2002.

Barish, Jonas. *The Antitheatrical Prejudice*. Berkeley, CA: University of California Press, 1981.

Berlin, Isaiah. "The Originality of Machiavelli." In *The Proper Study of Mankind: An Anthology of Essays*, edited by Henry Hardy and Roger Hausheer, 269–326. New York: Farrar, Straus & Giroux, 2012.

Cassirer, Ernst. *The Myth of the State*. New Haven, CT: Yale University Press, 1946.

Chiapelli, Fredi. *Studi sul Linguaggio del Machiavelli*. Florence, IT: F. Le Monnier, 1969.

Cochrane, Eric W. "Machiavelli 1940–1960." *Journal of Modern History* 33 (1961)113–36.

Cranz, F. Edward. *Nicholas of Cusa in the Renaissance*. Aldershot, UK: Ashgate Variorum, 2000.

50. Ellul, *Technological System*, 12, 46, 112 and Ellul, *Presence of the Kingdom*, 55.

51. Ellul, *Technological System*, 119.

52. Schmitt, *Dictatorship*, 6; McCormick, *Carl Schmitt's Critique of Liberalism*, 131.

53. Singleton, "The Perspective of Art," 180; McCanles *The Discourse of Il Principe*, 105–6 (emphasis original); Barish *The Antitheatrical Prejudice*, 97–98; Montanari , *La Poesia del Machiavelli*, 69; see Shaw, *Illusions of Freedom*, 6, quoting Carl Mitcham: "technology . . . is largely an unthinking activity."

———. *Reorientations of Western Thought from Antiquity to the Renaissance.* Aldershot, UK: Ashgate Variorum, 2006.

———. *Technology and Modern Reason.* New London, CT: De Litteris, 1980.

Croce, Benedetto. *Politics and Morals.* London: Allen & Unwin, 1945.

Ellul, Jacques. *Histoire de la Propagande.* Paris: Presses Universitaires de France, 1967.

———. *The Humiliation of the Word.* Translated by Joyce Main Hanks. Grand Rapids: Eerdmans, 1985.

———. *Perspectives on Our Age: Jacques Ellul Speaks on His Life and Work.* Edited by William H. Vanderburg. New York: House of Anansi, 2011.

———. *The Political Illusion.* Translated by Konrad Kellen. New York: Knopf, 1967.

———. *The Presence of the Kingdom.* Second Edition. Colorado Springs: Helmers & Howard, 1989.

———. *The Technological Bluff.* Translated by Geoffrey W. Bromiley. Grand Rapids: Eerdmans, 1990.

———. *The Technological Society.* Translated by John Wilkerson. New York: Vintage, 1964.

———. *The Technological System.* Translated by Joachim Neugroschel. New York: Continuum, 1980.

Ferroni, Giulio. "'Transformation' and 'Adaptation' in Machiavelli's *Mandragola*." In *Machiavelli and the Discourse of Literature,* edited by Albert Ascoli and Victoria Khan, 19–137. Ithaca, NY: Cornell University Press, 1993.

Greenwood, Richard. "Machiavelli and the Problem of Human Inflexibility." In *The Cultural Heritage of the Italian Renaissance: Essays in Honor of T.G. Griffith,* edited by Clive Griffiths and Robert Hastings, 196–214. Lewiston, NY: Edwin Mellen, 1993.

Hughes, Serge. "The Science of Machiavelli." *Commonweal* 376 (1951) 376–77.

Inglese, Giorgio. *Machiavelli Capitoli.* Rome: Bulzoni, 1981.

Lovekin, David. *Technique, Discourse, and Consciousness: An Introduction to the Philosophy of Jaques Ellul.* Bethlehem, PA: Lehigh University Press, 1991.

Machiavelli, Niccolò. *Tutte le Opere.* Edited by M. Martelli. Florence, IT: Sansoni, 1971.

———. *Opere, De Principatibus; Discorsi sopra la prima Deca di Tito Livio,* Volume 1, Tomes 1 & 2. Edited by R. Rinaldi. Turin, IT: UTET, 2006.

———. *Discourses on Livy.* Edited by Julian Bondanella and Peter Bondanella. New York: Oxford University Press, 1997.

———. *The Prince.* Indianapolis, IN: Hackett, 1976.

Mansfield, Harvey. *Machiavelli: Discourses on Livy.* Chicago: University of Chicago Press, 1996.

———. *Machiavelli: The Prince.* Chicago: University of Chicago Press, 1998.

———. *Machiavelli's Virtue.* Chicago: University of Chicago Press, 1998.

McCanles, Michael. *The Discourse of Il Principe.* Malibu, CA: Udena, 1985.

McCormick, John P. *Carl Schmitt's Critique of Liberalism: Against Politics as Technology.* Cambridge, UK: Cambridge University Press, 1999.

Montanari, Fausto. *La Poesia del Machiavelli.* Rome: Studium, 1968.

Moravia, Alberto. *L'Uomo come Fine e altri Saggi.* Milan, IT: Bompiani, 1964.

Musa, Mark. *Machiavelli's The Prince.* New York: St Martin's, 1964.

Najemy, John M. *Between Friends: Discourses of Power and Desire in the Machiavelli-Vettori Letters of 1513–1515.* Princeton, NJ: Princeton University Press, 1993.

———, ed. *The Cambridge Companion to Machiavelli.* Cambridge, UK: Cambridge University Press, 2010.

Raimondi, Ezio. "The Centaur and the Politician." In *Machiavelli and the Discourse of Literature*, A. Ascoli & V. Khan, 145–60. Ithaca, NY: Cornell University Press, 1993.

Ridolfi, Roberto. "Per un'Edizione Critica dell'Epistolario Machiavelliano. La lettera al Vettori del 29 Aprile 1513." *La Bibliofilia* 68 (1966) 31–50.

———. "I 'Ghiribizzi' al Soderini." *La Bibliofilia* 72 (1970) 53.

Ruffo-Fiore, Silvia. *Niccolò Machiavelli: An Annotated Bibliography of Modern Criticism and Scholarship*. New York: Greenwood, 1990.

Schmitt, Carl. *Dictatorship: From the Origin of the Modern Concept of Sovereignty to Proletarian Class Struggle*. Cambridge, UK: Polity, 2014.

Shaw, Jeffrey. *Illusions of Freedom: Thomas Merton and Jacques Ellul on Technology and the Human Condition*. Eugene OR: Pickwick, 2014.

Singleton, Charles. "The Perspective of Art." *Kenyon Review* 15 (1953) 169–89.

Strauss, Leo. *Thoughts on Machiavelli*. Seattle: University of Washington Press, 1958.

———. "The Three Waves of Modernity." In *An Introduction to Political Philosophy: Ten Essays*, edited by Hilail Gildin, 81–98. Detroit: Wayne State University Press, 1989.

Chapter 8

Two Views of Propaganda as a Form of Violence[1]

Jeffrey M. Shaw

> Reading Jacques Ellul's book *The Technological Society*. Great, full of firecrackers. A fine provocative book and one that really makes sense. . . . I wonder if all the Fathers [currently convened in Rome] are aware of all the implications of a technological society.[2]

WHAT WOULD THOMAS MERTON, a Roman Catholic monk, find so interesting in the writings of a French Protestant philosopher? What would compel Merton to mention Ellul's thoughts on the technological society in his journal? It turns out that Merton and Ellul actually have a great deal in common. Their respective views on the condition of society in the middle of the twentieth century are remarkably similar. This paper examines Merton's and Ellul's views on propaganda, some intellectual antecedents to their thinking, as well as the connections between Ellul's view of the concept of *technique* and Merton's view of the "mass man." For both Ellul and Merton, propaganda resembles violence; an insidious and pervasive phenomenon that is present in all societies.

While some Americans are familiar with Thomas Merton's writing, few are familiar with Jacques Ellul. A French philosopher of the mid-twentieth

---

1. This chapter is adapted from an article which originally appeared in the *Ellul Forum* 47 (2011). The basic premise of this chapter is expanded upon at length in Shaw, *Illusions of Freedom*.

2. Merton, *Dancing in the Water of Life*, 159–60.

century, Ellul has been described as both a scholar and a lay ecclesiastic.[3] Ellul's style is often considered verbose and dense, and his work should be approached as a whole rather than trying to figure out his worldview through reading only one or two of his major works. While it is not the intent in this paper to examine his worldview and his extensive writing on Christian faith, there is one topic that will need elaboration, and that is his concept of *technique*. This fundamental idea is central to most of Ellul's writing on modern society and on the condition of the modern world and man's place in it. In order to understand Ellul's central thesis, and also to understand the similarities between Merton's and Ellul's points of view regarding the condition of man in the modern world, it is first necessary to address the concept of technique.

Ellul's *Technique*

Ellul defines *technique* as "the totality of methods, rationally arrived at and having absolute efficiency in every field of human activity."[4] It is important to distinguish the idea of *technique* from technology itself. The products that result from advanced technology should be seen as only the most visible manifestation of technique. As Ellul clearly states, *technique* pervades every field of human endeavor, whether it be politics, medicine, or education. Propaganda is a phenomenon which is also subject to the demands of *technique*, but there is a symbiotic relationship between technique and propaganda. Ellul states, "I want to emphasize that the study of propaganda must be conducted within the context of the technological society. Propaganda, which is defined as information presented to compel individuals to act in a certain, preconceived manner, is called upon to solve problems created by technology, to play on maladjustments, and to integrate the individual into a technological world. In the midst of increasing mechanization and technological organization, propaganda is simply the means used to persuade man to submit with good grace."[5] It is along this line of thinking that we see the first comparisons between Ellul's thoughts on propaganda as contrasted to Merton.

3. Menninger, "Jacques Ellul: A Tempered Profile," 235.
4. Ellul, *The Technological Society*, xxv.
5. Ellul, *Propaganda*, xvii–xviii.

Merton's "Mass Man"

Thomas Merton is a well known Catholic author and monk. He is the author of *The Seven Storey Mountain* as well as numerous other books and stories. Like Ellul, Merton was concerned with the moral and spiritual state of the world and sought to not only explain how man had come to such a state, but how to transcend the situation as well.

While Merton never met Ellul or corresponded with him directly, there are citations in Merton's journals that reference the idea of technique, as well as numerous topics in Merton's writing that correlate quite well with the concept of technique in general. Merton's views on propaganda—its nature and its effect on modern society—are quite similar to Ellul's.

While Ellul presents his idea of technique as the primary obstacle to human fulfillment, Merton presents the idea of the "mass man" in many of his works. The mass man is essentially one that has surrendered the autonomy of a thinking individual for the comforts and conveniences of the modern world. In other words, mass man can be seen as the man or woman unknowingly cast into an allotted position in society based on the unseen and all powerful demands of technique. Merton says of this person "The inner life of the mass man, alienated and leveled in the existential sense, is a dull, collective routine of popular fantasies maintained in existence by the collective dream that goes on, without interruption, in the mass media."[6]

What role does Merton ascribe to propaganda? Much like Ellul, he sees propaganda as conditioning man to accept the reality of his condition as mass man. Merton believes that "action is not governed by moral reason but by political expediency and the demands of technology—translated into simple abstract forms of propaganda."[7] He goes on to say that this propaganda conditions the mass of men and women to react in a certain way to various stimuli.

Merton mentions Ellul specifically in *Conjectures of a Guilty Bystander*. Referring to propaganda, Merton states that "Jacques Ellul shows that a mass of factual and correct information can, even if not illogically presented, have the same effect as completely false and irrational propaganda."[8] While Ellul and Merton both spend some time in their respective writing dealing with particular forms of propaganda, such as Communist and

6. Merton, *Mystics and Zen Masters,* 268.

7. Merton, *Conjectures of a Guilty Bystander,* 65.

8. Ibid., 236.

Capitalist propaganda, not to mention Nazi propaganda, it is in a general, all encompassing propaganda that is found in the mass media, such as the press, television, and through advertising that the similarities between Ellul and Merton on the topic of propaganda are most pronounced. Both Ellul and Merton share the idea that man cannot choose to disregard the message that is continually broadcast through propaganda. According to Merton, one of the primary reasons for this is that in the West, it is customary to assume that technological progress is seen only as something inherently good, as well as *inevitable*.[9] The idea that technological progress is inevitable is congruent with Ellul's explanation of automatism as a defining characteristic of technique. Ellul explains that technique is self-augmenting, as he writes in *The Technological Society*, "let no one say that man is the agent of technical progress . . . and that it is he who chooses among possible techniques. He can decide *only* in favor of the technique that gives maximum efficiency. But this is not choice."[10]

Merton shares a similar observation concerning freedom and choice when he states, "Because we live in a womb of collective illusion, our freedom remains abortive. They can never be used. We are prisoners of a process, a dialectic of false promises and real deceptions ending in futility."[11] Merton's view that technical progress is inevitable is similar to Ellul's view that technique determines its own path, irrespective of man's choices. Regarding choice, "Merton saw the effect of the secular myth of progress as a surrendering of human freedom and spontaneity to an unseen yet pervasive principle of efficiency that promises to fulfill our desires if we accept our roles as cogs in the machine."[12] Here we see similarities to not only the role of technique as defined by Ellul, but also the notion that our desires are fulfilled for us, and that it is through propaganda that these desires are both manufactured and made known to us.

Merton hoped for some degree of control over technology. He recorded in his diary that "those who foresee and work for a social order—a transformation of the world—[must work] according to these principles: primacy of the person . . . control of technology . . . etc."[13] Control of technology can be seen in this light as either the freedom from the demands of

9. Merton, *Turning Towards the World*, 4.

10. Ellul, *Technological Society*, 80.

11. Merton, *Raids on the Unspeakable*, 14.

12. Kelly, "Thomas Merton's Critique of Technological Civilization," 5.

13. Merton, *Turning Towards the World*, 10.

technique, or a refusal to continue to participate in the mindless consumption so prevalent in American society as Merton goes on to say in the same diary entry, "primacy of wisdom and love, against materialism, hedonism, etc."[14]

Merton's reading of Hannah Arendt's *The Human Condition* influenced his thinking on the relationship between man and technology. While it is sometimes difficult, as we have seen, to distinguish in Merton's writing between his opposition to the products of technology and the process of technological "progress," it is clear in his reflection on Arendt that his opposition is to the process itself. This line of thinking more clearly parallels Ellul. Merton notes in his journal that Arendt believes that "Being has been replaced by process. The process is everything. Modern man sees only how to fit without friction into productive processes and in this he finds 'happiness.'"[15] This thought is remarkably congruent with Ellul's observation on the effects of technique although there is one major difference. Merton seems to imply that man has chosen to fit himself into the process whereas Ellul would argue that technique molds man into the process unknowingly. For Ellul, technique determines its own path, whereas Merton, in his reflection on *The Human Condition,* seems to imply that man has chosen to go along with process willingly, yet without adequately reflecting on the price he has paid.

Sōren Kierkegaard's writing is an antecedent to the thought of both Ellul and Merton. In *The Present Age,* Kierkegaard, a Danish philosopher of the mid-nineteenth century, presents the concept of leveling. Examining this idea will lead us to conclude that both Ellul and Merton have incorporated some of its basic tenets into their own thinking on the condition of man and society in their age, which is about a century after Kierkegaard.

Kierkegaard as Antecedent

Kierkegaard refers to leveling as an "abstract power."[16] He also refers to his times as an "age of advertisement and publicity."[17] The notion of advertising is important to the process of leveling, through which man is forced into a herd-like existence, devoid of passion and individuality. Describing

14. Ibid.
15. Ibid., 11.
16. Kierkegaard, *The Present Age,* 52.
17. Ibid., 35.

the forces responsible for the process of leveling and its results, Kierkegaard states that "the Press is an abstraction . . . which in conjunction with the passionless and reflective character of the age produces that abstract phantom: a public which in turn is really the leveling power."[18] Merton picks up on this theme in his own writing when he states, as we have already seen from his quote in *Mystics and Zen Masters*, that "the inner life of the mass man, alienated and leveled in the existential sense, is a dull, collective routine of popular fantasies maintained in existence by the collective dream that goes on, without interruption, in the mass media."[19]

Kierkegaard makes a point to stress that his age is lacking in passion. Both Ellul and Merton also make reference to their societies lacking passion. Merton says that Western society is in the grip of pseudo-passion, "fabricated in the imagination and centered on fantasies."[20] Ellul claims that in his view, technique "attacks man, impairs the source of his vitality, and takes away his mystery."[21] In presenting an idea that corresponds to both Kierkegaard's leveling process and to the idea of technique as a force which will act on all men, Merton states that "the abstract leveling process, that self-combustion of the human race produced by the friction which arises when an individual ceases to exist as singled out by religion, is bound to continue like a trade wind until it consumes everything."[22] Ellul does not specifically reference any of Kierkegaard's philosophy or his ideas in general in *Propaganda*, but he does make reference to him in *The Technological Society*. He states that "In the middle of the nineteenth century, when technique had hardly begun to develop, another voice was raised in prophetic warning against it. The voice was Kierkegaard's. But his warnings . . . were not heeded. They were too close to the truth."[23]

Conclusion

We can see that examining Jacques Ellul's and Thomas Merton's writing on propaganda, it would appear that we have little hope of recapturing anything resembling an authentic human life outside of the bonds of the mass.

18. Ibid., 64.
19. Merton, *Mystics and Zen Masters*, 268.
20. Merton, *Conjectures of a Guilty Bystander*, 32.
21. Ellul, *Technological Society*, 415.
22. Merton, *Mystics and Zen Masters*, 264.
23. Ellul, *Technological Society*, 55.

However, at least one of the two writers offers us hope. Thomas Merton believes that through *kenosis* and *metanoia*, one can begin to escape from the bonds imposed on society by the twin pillars of spiritual malaise and the increasing demands of modernization, secularization, and "progress." *Kenosis,* or the self-emptying that one finds in the mystical traditions, is one of the great lessons that the West can learn from the East. Kenosis is an ego-shattering practice.[24] *Metanoia* is a Greek word for the concept of total personal transformation.[25] Emphasizing either of these practices and focusing on spiritual renewal through contemplation, one can transcend the mass. However, Ellul offers more pessimistic view. Without delving into his entire body of theological writing, which does in fact offer the reader the possibility of escape from *technique,* the diagnosis offered in *The Technological Society* is a grim one indeed. His assessment of *technique* is more of an autopsy of modern society than any kind of remedy for escaping the grip that *technique* holds on all of us. Concerning the completion of the edifice of technical society, he says that "it will not be a universal concentration camp, because it will be guilty of no atrocity. It will not be insane, because everything will be ordered . . . we shall have nothing more to lose, and nothing to win . . . we shall be rewarded with everything our hearts ever desire . . . and the supreme luxury of the society of technical necessity will be to grant the bonus of useless revolt and of an acquiescent smile."[26]

Jacques Ellul and Thomas Merton share many similarities when it comes to their views on the nature of propaganda. They both see propaganda as a force that compels man to accept his position in a technological society, as in Ellul, or as the mass man, as per Merton. They can both be seen to have intellectual antecedents in the philosophy of Sören Kierkegaard. While Ellul offers us no hope of liberating ourselves from the clutches of propaganda, Merton offers us at least some consolation in the form of ascetic withdrawal and moral renewal.

References

Dekar, Paul. "What the Machine Produces and What the Machine Destroys: Thomas Merton on Technology." *The Merton Annual* 17 (2004) 216–34.

24. Nouwen, *Thomas Merton: Contemplative Critic,* 83.
25. Dekar, "What the Machine Produces and What the Machine Destroys," 219.
26. Ellul, *Technological Society,* 427.

Ellul, Jacques. *Propaganda*. Translated by Konrad Kellen & Jean Lerner. New York: Alfred A. Knopf, 1965.

———. *The Technological Society*. Translated by John Wilkerson. New York: Vintage Books, 1964.

Kelly, Christopher J. "Thomas Merton's Critique of Technological Civilization." *Ellul Forum* 21 (1998) 3–13.

Kierkegaard, Søren. *The Present Age*. Translated by Alexander Dru. New York: Harper & Row, 1962.

Menninger, David C. "Jacques Ellul: A Tempered Profile." *The Review of Politics* 37 (1975) 235–46.

Merton, Thomas. *Conjectures of a Guilty Bystander*. Garden City, NY: Doubleday, 1966.

———. *Dancing in the Waters of Life*. Edited by Robert E. Daggy. San Francisco: Harper Collins, 1967.

———. *Mystics and Zen Masters*. New York: Noonday Press, 1961.

———. *Seeds of Destruction*. New York: Farrar, Straus, and Giroux, 1961.

———. *Turning Towards the World*. Edited by Victor A. Kramer. San Francisco: Harper Collins, 1996.

Nouwen, Henri M. *Thomas Merton: Contemplative Critic*. San Francisco: Harper & Row, 1972.

Shaw, Jeffrey M. *Illusions of Freedom: Thomas Merton and Jacques Ellul on Technology and the Human Condition*. Eugene, OR: Pickwick, 2014.

Chapter 9

Propaganda as Psychic Violence

Peter K. Fallon

IN HIS CLASSIC 1965 work on mass persuasion in the technological society, *Propaganda: The Formation of Men's Attitudes*, Jacques Ellul provides us with both schematic and user's manual of the propaganda system. He outlines the intricate and complex interdependent mechanisms through which the technical system imposes control, emphasizes how those different mechanisms act to reinforce one another, explains the necessity of such mechanisms—for both the state and the individual—and the inevitability of such a complex system in a mass society. He differentiates and describes for the reader the different types and levels of propaganda; political, sociological, agitation, integration, vertical, horizontal, rational and irrational, and explains precisely how, where, when, and why each of these comes into play in political, social, and economic life. And he contrasts the dominant post-modern propaganda system of the technological society with the ideologically-driven propagandas of the early-modern and modern eras.

The propagandas of the past were propagandas of violence and coercion; and the coercion administered—whether by a Soviet Communist, a Nazi information minister, or a Catholic Inquisitor—was always justified by and based on a demand to adhere to an ideological "truth," whether one was inclined toward that "truth" or not. It is interesting to note that the success of these propagandas was as much indebted to the KGB and the gulags, the Schutzstaffel (SS) and the death camps, and the Inquisitors and the *auto de fe* as it was to the persuasive power of the message or the credibility of the communicators. These were propagandas backed up by physical force and violence, and it is legitimate to wonder how effective these older forms might have been, absent the threat of torture, physical injury, suffering, and death.

In these older forms of societal organization, ideology preceded propaganda, it motivated it, rationalized it, gave it meaning and purpose, and as a result the propaganda flowed from the ideology, spreading it to the mass. Consequently, we have, in the past, witnessed frequent "propaganda wars," each propaganda being rationalized by its own distinct ideology,[1] whether communist, capitalist, fascist, or Nazi. But the propaganda of the technological society no longer flows from the ideology, nor does ideology—*any ideology*—precede it. Rather, Ellul tells us, there is a new relationship between propaganda and ideology. Individual ideologies, in the technologically developed world, are in fact little more than side shows, evidence of subjective, surface differences of opinion about relatively trivial matters that have no real impact on the over-arching, dominant, and monolithic message of the technological society: *technique itself*. Technique is the reigning ideology of the technological society, and propaganda is nothing more than technique; propaganda no longer follows ideology but, rather, is ideology itself.[2] It is its own content. In McLuhanian terms, the medium is the message.

The values of technique—productivity, profit, speed, consumption, convenience, maximization, etc., but above all *efficiency*—are also the values of the technical system of which propaganda is a central and supporting part. And while the appearance of a social dynamism remains—one group in society may be aggrieved at another group's perceived preferential treatment, or feel that their own path to full assimilation is impeded by discrimination, or squabble over wages or working conditions—*no one* questions the righteousness of the technical values and all groups are either enjoying, or waiting and expecting to enjoy, their fruits. And, since it is the most efficient thing for the system to do, eventually every group becomes assimilated and enjoys their material comforts. In the meantime, those subjective, superficial differences among different social groupings provide an illusion of diversity of thought and opinion and, pervading the airwaves and fiber optical cables of the technological communication infrastructure, become nothing more than additional sources of entertaining content to be

1. Ellul, *Propaganda*, 194.
2. Ibid., 198.

discussed, debated, and argued over while posing no significant threat to the stability of the state or the society.

And so the systematic propaganda of the technological society yields a surprisingly cohesive mass, diverse on a surface level but deeply homogeneous in its core values, attitudes, myths, and beliefs. The rewards of technique are demonstrable and tangible, and everyone wants to share in them. This is a different kind of propaganda, a post-modern propaganda that needs no gulags, no death camps, no torture chambers to produce what Noam Chomsky calls "the spectacular achievements" of contemporary propaganda.[3] No shots are fired, no poison gases are used, no lash breaks the skin of a single person's back. On the contrary, the systematic propaganda of the technological society succeeds by inflicting *pleasure and amusement* rather than pain.

It is my argument in this chapter that propaganda represents a form of violence and that this violence takes its toll on the group upon whom it is inflicted. We must be careful, however, not to take this argument too far or in the wrong direction. Certainly the type of violence I'm referring to can't be equal to the violence we see far too often in our various media, the kind of violence that leaves people mangled, maimed, helpless, dead. The type of violence I'm referring to is not a rape, or the lopping off of a hand, or a beheading, or a war, it is not torture, it is not murder; but it is violence none the less, a different kind of violence, a quieter, subtler, more nuanced sort of violence. Indeed, I suspect many will disregard my argument entirely because they see violence in a monolithic way, in stark contrast to a condition called "non-violence," devoid of shades of gray. So I heed Jacques Ellul's advice that "the first thing the Christian must do regarding violence is to perceive exactly what violence is."[4]

Defining Terms

The Oxford English Dictionary lists several meanings for the word:

> Violence: noun; 1 The exercise of physical force so as to cause injury or damage to a person, property, etc; physically violent behavior or activity; 2 The state or quality of being violent in action

3. Indeed, it is not even necessary to jail or torture political dissidents like a Chomsky or a Howard Zinn in the technological society; propaganda simply ignores them and we rarely if ever hear about them.

4. Ellul, *Violence*, 84.

or effect; great force or strength in operation; vehemence, severity, intensity; 3 Strength or intensity of emotion; fervor, passion; 4
The action or an act of constraining or forcing unnatural change
upon something; *spec.* (a) misinterpretation or misapplication of
a word.[5]

It is clear that the first definition will not suit the purposes of the present argument; this definition represents what we generally think of when
we hear the word "violence" and I would not want to try to equate mass
persuasion with physical harm or offend the sensibilities of those who have
actually undergone the trauma of physical violence.

The second definition is equally unsuitable, though for different reasons. "Violence" in this sense is metaphorical (a "violent storm," a "violent
reaction") and doesn't capture the essence of the violence I wish to describe.

The third definition comes close to being useful, as propaganda can
certainly evoke strong emotional response and incite violence. Ultimately,
however, this definition focuses on the reaction to something rather than
on violent action itself.

But the fourth definition is important to note and useful to the argument; we do not need to conceive of violence as being limited to damage
to property, physical injury, or death. Violence also implies *constraining or
forcing unnatural change* on others, and this sort of coercion can include
the misuse of language and symbols. Referring once again to the OED, we
find the following among the various definitions of the word *propaganda*:
"Information, especially of a biased or misleading nature, used to promote
or publicize a particular political cause or point of view."[6] Misusing language in order to constrain another's thoughts and/or behaviors, or to force
a change of thoughts and behaviors on one whom otherwise would think
and act differently is characteristic, then, of *both* propaganda and violence.

The discerning reader is not, at this point, entirely persuaded. This
is completely understandable. We've already determined that the kind of
"violence" to which I compare propaganda bears no relation to the type
of violence that leaves people bloodied, disfigured, or dead. We've already
seen that in the new form of propaganda characteristic of the technological
society physical coercion, threats of violence, and *physical* violence itself are
all rare and for the most part unnecessary. And as we shall see in looking at

5. *The Shorter Oxford English Dictionary*, s.v. "Violence," 3:535.
6. Ibid., s.v. "Propaganda," 2:368.

Ellul's critique, people living in an environment of systematic propaganda come to enjoy it and even crave it. How bad, then, could it be?

Ellul on Violence and the State

Ellul claims that "every state is founded on violence and cannot maintain itself save by and through violence."[7] Common sense tells us that he is correct about that. The *social contract*, whether represented by Hobbes's "Leviathan," Locke's "pursuit of life, liberty, and property," or Rousseau's "fall from grace," implies the constant and continual surrender of individual rights and sovereignty, generation after generation, to the state in return for protection from violence and lawlessness. While Hobbes sees this contract as inherently beneficial to the common good and order, Locke as a thing useful in the *pursuit* of the good, and Rousseau as no more than a necessary—and regrettable—evil, all agree fundamentally on this point: the presence of or potential for violence is constantly with us, whether in the form of police and prisons, state militias, or the military. We are, in a sense, coerced into civilization.

But in a more literal (as opposed to philosophical) way, violence is a very real part of the history of most civil states. "The state is established by violence—the French, American, Communist, Francoist revolutions. Invariably there is violence at the start."[8] Violence appears not only at the inception of the state, but remains an integral part. "Now how does a government stay in power? By violence, simply by violence. It has to eliminate its enemies, set up new structures; and that, of course, can be done only by violence."[9] Violence, or its threat, first establishes and then maintains the stability and proper order of the state. "Domestically, too, the state uses violence. Before it does anything else it must establish order—such is the first great rule for states."[10]

So it seems that there is a presumed threat of violence in all civil states that is necessary (or, as Ellul says, "in the order of necessity") for the ordered survival of the state. This violence pervades not only the political dimension of the technological society, but its economic and social dimensions as well.

7. Ellul, *Violence*, 84.
8. Ibid.
9. Ibid., 85.
10. Ibid.

"Violence" in the Technological Society

The violence that accrues in civil societies that develop complex technologies is, of course, far greater—if often more subtle—than that of less developed, more traditional, more "organic" cultures.[11] A perceived threat of violence pervades our lives and we live with a constant fear that violence will rear its ugly head and disrupt the peace we have managed to achieve and maintain in our homes, our communities, and our minds. We fear the (potentially violent) intentions of others—other nations, other ideologies, other races, other people. We fear the (often violent) brutality of nature— the floods, droughts, fires, lightning strikes, heart attacks. We fear aging and sickness and death. These are existential fears. We also, however, fear influences that lurk far below the level of existential threat. We fear poverty, for instance (a condition that arises only in an environment of mass prosperity; or, as Marshall McLuhan once said, "affluence creates poverty"). We fear being "left behind" or looked down on by others. We fear being "out of the loop." We fear living meaningless lives. According to Ellul,

---

11. There is a great deal of controversy over this point, which is why I have chosen my words ("far greater—if often more subtle") as carefully as I have. Many scholars and commentators in the field of anthropology argue that "primitive" human societies were far more violent than "civilized" societies. For example, see Keeley, *War Before Civilization* and Pinker, *The Blank Slate,* especially 254 & 306–36 for a pointed argument on the human predisposition for violence. Others, however, argue the opposite. R. Brian Ferguson, for example, argues in *Pinker's List: Exaggerating Prehistoric War Mortality* (in Douglas P. Fry, ed., *War, Peace, and Human Nature: The Convergence of Evolutionary and Cultural Views* [Oxford; Oxford University Press, 2013], ch. 7, pp. 112–131) that Pinker's data regarding war deaths in primitive societies versus 20th century Europe and the US is "massaged" and presented in such a way as to support his own prejudices. For example, Ferguson criticizes Pinker's citing of the archeological remains of the victims of a massacre at Crow Creek, South Dakota in the 14th century. That number represented (an estimated) 60 percent of the population living in that area at the time, a proportion of murder victims from a general population unthinkable in the current age. But that perspective may be entirely the problem. In the 14th century, the Earth's population was about 350 million people and 486 deaths out of a total of 810 people living in a single locality is frightening. In the 20th century, by contrast, the population rose from about 2 billion to 6 billion people. Even granting the point that per capita deaths by warfare and violence has declined, the estimated 200 million people who died in 20th century warfare or political violence (less than 1 percent of the Earth's population) simply cannot be compared with 486 deaths, no matter how violent. As Ellul points out, technologies do not introduce problems into human life unknown before their invention; they introduce problems of scale. What could once be achieved on the level of the individual or the small group—for good or evil—can now be achieved on massive levels.

> Anxiety is perhaps the most widespread psychological trait in our society. Many studies indicate that fear is one of the strongest and most prevalent feelings in our society. Of course, man has good reasons to be afraid—of Communist subversion, revolution, Fascism, H-bombs, conflict between East and West, unemployment, sickness. On the one hand, the number of dangers is increasing and, because of the news media, man is more aware of them; on the other, religious beliefs, which allowed man to face fear, have disappeared almost entirely. Man is disarmed in the face of the perils threatening him, and is increasingly alarmed by these perils because he keeps reading about them.[12]

Life in the tightly-structured, highly-connected, information-rich, spatially- and temporally-compressed technological society—so much more than in earlier, more traditional societal forms—imposes a sort of *psychic trauma* on those who have no choice but to live within its boundaries. Again, Ellul adds,

> Psychologists and sociologists are aware of the great problem of adjusting the normal man to a technological environment—to the increasing pace, the working hours, the noise, the crowded cities, the tempo of work, the housing shortage, and so on. Then there is the difficulty of accepting the never-changing daily routine, the lack of personal accomplishment, the absence of an apparent meaning in life, the family insecurity provoked by these living conditions, the anonymity of the individual in the big cities and at work. The individual is not equipped to face these disturbing, paralyzing, traumatic influences.[13]

Propaganda in the technological society strips the individual of his own individuality by making him a part of an indissoluble mass. It strips the individual of individuality by inhibiting her critical thought and personal judgment. It strips the individual of individuality by making her responsible for a "public opinion" which has no power to drive or direct government, even though she has been assured it has. Propaganda imposes a *societal neurosis* which, under the influence of propaganda, is perceived by its object—*the mass individual*—to be perfectly "normal."[14] We are no longer organic individuals; we are creatures formed—emotionally, psychologically, spiritually—in the crucible of technology, human manifestations

12. Ellul, *Propaganda*, 153.

13. Ibid., 143.

14. Ibid., 163–68.

of technique, and our "natural" cognitive and affective processes—even our autonomic functions—are programmed to respond to the sensory data that come to us, not directly through our senses, but through the mediation of technology in our mass-manufactured "reality."

> Man is capable of outbursts of passion and violence. It does not seem that those sources of vital energy which might be summarized as sexuality, spirituality, and capacity for feeling have been impaired. But every time these forces attempt to assert themselves, they are flung against a ring of iron with which technique surrounds and localizes them. Moreover, technique attacks man, impairs the sources of his vitality, and takes away his mystery. We have seen that one of the objectives of certain human techniques is to rob him of this mystery. And men must and do react instinctively and spiritually to the aggression of technique.[15]

As a consequence, the object of mass propaganda—*the propagandee* — finds himself in a most uncomfortable position: alienated not only from himself, his conscience, his true individuality, his free will; but also from his actual (as opposed to virtual) community—his neighbors, his friends, his workmates, his peers, and the strangers he passes on the street. He is closest, and clings most desperately, not to the human members of his actual community, but to the virtual members of his mass-manufactured "reality": the characters he "knows" from television, the celebrities whose escapades he follows on the Internet, the "friends" he's never met on Facebook, the popular gossip he shares "dirt" with via text messages. These are the predictable and dependable constituents of his life. His most intimate interactions are not with human beings, but with mediated versions of human beings: images, avatars, icons, profile pictures, and disembodied data. These are his constant companions. The propagandee thus finds his every waking moment mediated by some technology—or in the case of the much-vaunted "multi-tasker," by a variety of different technologies. To the propagandee—*the mass individual*—this is all entirely normal. And all social creatures can tolerate abnormality only so long; we crave the normal, become dependent on it.

This scenario Ellul describes is the nature of life in the technological society. This is, or has become, in fact, the new nature. The technological milieu is the "natural" habitat of technological man; to propose a world with limited technologies seems patently unnatural. There is no questioning

15. Ellul, *Technological Society*, 415.

technology's legitimacy or its reality; to do so poses an existential threat to both the technical system and to all those who live within it; even worse, it is impractical and inefficient. *This is just the way it is.* This is the way it is meant to be. This is what is right. This is life. This is "natural." *Of course* you should have a smartphone! It's important to be connected to the rest of the world. *Of course* technology should hold a central place in education! How can our kids get jobs if they are unfamiliar with the newest technologies? *Of course* constant change is a permanent dimension of our society! It's called *progress*, and the nation that avoids progress is doomed to stagnation in an imperfect present. *Of course* businesses must outsource their labor to developing countries! It's more efficient and profitable to be competitive. *Of course* market forces are objective! You can't question the wisdom of a majority of people who choose one thing over another. *Of course* technology is good! Would you want to live in a world without, for instance, medical technologies?

This mindset of technological "normalcy" comes, however, at a significant price. Ellul stated,

> We still do not know the ultimate effects of these transformations on the human being. We have only begun to study them. Precisely what is modified in man by this violent upheaval of every element of his environment? We do not know. But we do know that violent modifications have taken place, and we have a foreboding of them in the development of neuroses and in the new behaviors with which contemporary literature acquaints us. In ceasing to be himself, modern man bears testimony to these phenomena not only when he suffers anxiety but even when he is happy. For the last decade scientific studies have been accumulating which demonstrate man's psychological, moral, and even biological incapacity to adapt in any real way to the milieu technique has created for him.[16]

And yet there is a piece of the technological man that hearkens back to the pre-technologically complex days, that remains wholly human, that maintains the "vital energy" Ellul refers to, that refuses to surrender passion, that longs to embrace some inscrutable mystery, that rejects the logic of the senses, or reason, or technique, and yearns for a life of intuition and imagination—*unmediated by technology*. In the days prior to the establishment of

16. Ibid., 331.

the fully-technologized society, the state needed to be prepared to step in, unafraid to use violence or the threat of violence. This is because

> The individual is not by himself rational enough to accept what is necessary to the machines. He rebels too easily. He requires an agency to constrain him, and the state [has] to play this role . . . Thus, the techniques of the state—military, police, administrative, and political—[make] their appearance. Without them, all the rest would have been no more than faint hopes unable to attain maximum development. They intermingled, necessitating one another, and all of them necessitated by the economy.[17]

But violence, as we have seen, is a symptom of un-maximized efficiency and will not be assimilated comfortably in a highly-technologized milieu. Violence (and the unspoken threat of violence) must be minimized in the technological society and the ultimate impetus toward order and stability must be imbued in, and flow from, the mass, and "it soon became evident that such external action was insufficient. A great effort was required of the individual, and this effort he could not make unless he was genuinely convinced, not merely constrained. He must be made to yield his heart and will, as he had yielded his body and brain. And so the techniques of propaganda, education, and psychic manipulation came to reinforce the others."[18] Nor are technological man's interactions with his economic world untouched by technique. The values of the technological society—productivity, profit, speed, consumption, convenience, maximization, etc., but above all *efficiency*—suffuse technical man and his entire culture and provide a context for his own values, attitudes, beliefs, and behaviors. And those values, attitudes, beliefs, and behaviors reflect the violence of technique and of the systematic propaganda which supports it. Ellul noted that "the competition that goes with the much-touted system of free enterprise is, in a word, an economic 'war to the knife,' an exercise of sheer violence that, so far, the law has not been able to regulate. In this competition 'the best man wins'—and the weaker, more moral, more sensitive men necessarily lose."[19] Home life, personal life, social life, the "life of the mind" (such as it is), the spiritual life, the economic life—all tumble before the power of technique. Looking at Abraham Maslow's "hierarchy of needs," we can see that every ascending step on the ladder, every need is now satisfied through technique. This is

17. Ibid.
18. Ibid., 115.
19. Ellul, *Violence*, 86.

not, we should acknowledge, an entirely negative thing, for human beings have always used technology. It is one of the defining characteristics of our species to create and use tools to fulfill fundamental needs. But the "needs" fulfilled by technology were once fairly limited to those lower on Maslow's hierarchy—food, clothing, shelter, water, etc. (physiological and security needs); the higher we move up Maslow's pyramid—to love and belonging, esteem, and self-actualization—the greater we see the growing influence of the propaganda of the technological society on our lives. Our friendships and familial relationships are more and more mediated; even our sexuality and sexual lives cannot escape technique. Our self-esteem is judged—by ourselves as well as by others—by our assimilation (or lack of assimilation) into the technical milieu. Our morality—our basic sense of right and wrong—is based on the values of technology, our creativity is dependent on our knowledge of and utility with tools, our capacity for problem-solving useless in the absence of technology.

It may be pure hyperbole to hear the common pop culture lamentation, "I simply couldn't live without my (fill in the technology of your choice: smartphone, tablet, Tivo, etc.)." But it may also be true—to the extent that all myths are true to those who believe them (this principle is, of course, at the very heart of propaganda)—that technological man is completely dependent on his technology. We are captivated—held captive—by our toolish, toyish technologies; we are enthralled by them, held under their mighty power, slaves to their allure. If, as the late Jesuit Fr. John Culkin of Fordham University said, "We shape our tools and thereafter they shape us," it appears that the user is being used. [20] The holder of the tool is, in fact, held by it.

Systematic Propaganda as a Form of "Stockholm Syndrome"

This is a most unnatural and pathogenic situation for a human being to find himself in: to be controlled but to believe oneself, at the same time, to be in a position of control. I would like to suggest an analogy to the situation described in the last several pages, that being the *Stockholm Syndrome*. I suggest this analogy not with any claim of any empirical correlation between being held hostage and living in an environment of constant, continuous, and continual propaganda, but in a metaphorical sense, in a heuristic spirit, that we might notice some curious similarities between the two situations.

20. A quote frequently—but incorrectly—attributed to Marshall McLuhan.

The term "Stockholm syndrome" refers to a number of psychological symptoms frequently evident in people who have been kidnapped or taken hostage. The syndrome was defined by one of its earliest observers as "a disorder whereby abductees bond with or express loyalty toward their captors in an effort to save their lives or make their ordeal more tolerable."[21] It is a condition sheathed in controversy; some researchers point out that sensationalist mass media have tended to ascribe the syndrome to inappropriate cases,[22] that "existing literature is of limited research value and does little to support 'Stockholm syndrome' as a psychiatric diagnosis,"[23] and that 'Stockholm syndrome' is not a recognized Medical Subject Heading."[24] Others note that, given the uncertainty of the syndrome's place in psychiatric medicine, its increasing application (again, frequently in the mass media) to situations beyond kidnapping and hostage-taking (e.g., abusive relationships, gender discrimination, racial politics, etc.) reinforces a culture of victimhood.[25]

Yet, for all the ambiguity surrounding the syndrome,[26] there is little doubt in the psychiatric field of its existence. Researchers have determined that three factors must be at work in order for the Stockholm syndrome to become evident in victims:

- Forced captivity is long-term rather than brief.

- Captors remain in constant contact with only the captives (no outside contact).

- Captors treat captives well or at least don't hurt them; captives abused or harmed by captors typically feel anger toward them and do not usually develop the syndrome.[27]

21. Strentz, *The Stockholm Syndrome*, 137–50.

22. Namnyak, "'Stockholm syndrome': psychiatric diagnosis or urban myth?" 4.

23. Ibid.

24. Ibid.

25. Adorjan, *Stockholm Syndrome as Vernacular Resource*, 454–74.

26. Much of the ambiguity is attributable to the fact that whatever data we have for understanding the Stockholm syndrome come from accounts of actual hostage situations; each of these situations has differed significantly in its context (e.g., where did it occur, how many captors/hostages were involved, what was the level of threat involved, etc.). Ethics (and institutional review boards) would prohibit the design of most experiments seeking greater understanding of the effects of such experiences on human beings.

27. Frey, *Stockholm Syndrome*, 4134–36.

If these conditions are met, we are likely to witness the following:

- Captives displaying negative feelings about those who might help them (e.g., police or other authorities).
- Captives displaying positive feelings toward their captor(s).
- Captors tending to the hostages' needs.[28]

It is interesting to note some of the similarities among these factors and characteristics and Ellul's description of systematic propaganda: the continual and continuous long-term nature of propaganda, the need to have no other frame of reference available to the propagandee than that of the propaganda system itself, the need for propaganda to deliver what the propagandee wants (facts, myths, information that makes the propagandee feel "safe" and "secure" in his environment, etc.), the need for propaganda not to "hurt" the propagandee (by lying or failing to deliver on promised benefits, etc.). Equally interesting are the results: technological man feels a kinship with the very entity that alienates him from nature, embraces a "reality" that not only is unlike the reality of authentic freedom, but would be loathsome to him in the absence of fear, identifies with the threatening power, sympathizes with it; technological man is repulsed by anyone who would "help" him recover from a technical captivity, looks on such a person as a dangerous threat rather than a friend.

Conclusion

In one of the most important books of the twentieth century, Victor E. Frankl recounts his many months of captivity in a Nazi concentration camp. What a desolate and hopeless place it was, a place where you lived in the presence of violence, breathed in the stench of death, where your wife, parents, children, were taken from you, where you or your bunk mate might disappear or be murdered without a moment's notice; a place where all the previous certainties of life simply disappeared, a limbo, a purgatory with no hope of salvation, only of death. A place with no apparent way to make sense of any of its being or your place in its being—except to die. Those who could not make sense of their lives within the horror of the death camps were the first to give up their will to live, and quickly died.

28. Ibid.

Those who could imagine something—*anything*—to live for, fought to stay alive as long as they could.

Frankl reminded us that the human species is defined by self-conscious, responsible choices. The choices we make determine the people we are and the people we become as well as the lives we lead. As denizens of a technological society, we are surrounded and assaulted by messages and the information structures that deliver them to us. Each moment we have an opportunity—and, Frankl says, a responsibility—to consider those messages, to become and remain aware of the structures, and to respond in a way that enhances, rather than degrades our lived experiences. Man is a creature who either searches for meaning, or dies. Sometimes, however, the search is brief and half-hearted. We can, as most technological humans do, allow our cultures to impose mass-manufactured meaning on our lives (i.e., our beliefs, our attitudes, our values, our behaviors) and simply respond accordingly. Or we can struggle with the soulless machine to create our own meaning. "When we are no longer able to change a situation . . . we are challenged to change ourselves."[29] This is essentially the message Jacques Ellul provides, although not in the two critical works cited most prominently in this chapter, *The Technological Society* and *Propaganda*. This is the message of Ellul's *theology*—which ought to be read as a complement to his sociological and cultural criticism. Ellul wants us to be revolutionaries, to subvert the material powers that hold hostage our human spirit. But, he warns us, in order to be more than stereotypes of "the revolutionary," stamped with the meaning our mass culture imposes, we must be revolutionary *in a revolutionary way*, and our subversion must be personal and not social. If we are to someday change the world—*and there is no guarantee that such a day will ever come*—we must first fundamentally change ourselves. But how?

Ellul offers us some advice on how to subvert the power of the world and reclaim control over our lives and spirit. First, become *aware*, which

> means the refusal to accept appearances at face value, and of information for information's sake, the refusal of the abstract phenomenon, the refusal of the illusion given by present means, the consoling illusion of "progress," and of the improvement of situations and of men, by a sort of benevolent fatalism of history.[30]

29. Frankl, *Man's Search for Meaning*, 116.
30. Ellul, *Presence of the Kingdom*, 98.

We must fight back against the spiritual violence that keeps us from our true selves. We must reject ideologies, both old and new, shatter myths which support our self-surrender to technique, refuse to conform for conformity's sake and be conscious and responsible in all our actions.[31]

We must also develop a belief in, and the will to find, an objective reality beyond the mediated, televised, and streaming one, especially by discovering "the facts of the life led by the people who surround me,"[32] the actual, as opposed to the virtual inhabitants of our world. This is a spiritual rather than a social revolution, and will take place not on the level of the mass (and virtual reality), but on the human level. Ellul believed that we must "refuse energetically to be detached from this sphere, a level which is not very high, but is the only significant one. This means that first we must get rid of all evasion, in all its forms—in the ideal, in the future, in abstraction. We must no longer think of "men" in the abstract, but of my neighbor Mario."[33]

"We need a revolution," Ellul concludes, "in a world in which it has become impossible,"[34] a highly technologically developed world of the mass-manufactured, mass-marketed, and mass-distributed reality. "We need a rediscovery of the meaning of human activity, of the relation between means and ends, of their true place in a world which is given up to the love of power"[35] over material reality. The revolutionary spirit—the will to fight the violence of technique—demands that we acknowledge the fact that violence is a natural and normal part of society, that it dwells in what Ellul calls "the realm of necessity" "imposed on governors and governed, on rich and poor. If this realism scandalizes Christians, it is because they make the great mistake of thinking what is *natural* is *good* and what is *necessary* is *legitimate*."[36]

In considering violence to be part of the human condition dwelling in the realm of necessity, and acknowledging that fact, it might become possible to cease our attempts to avoid it. For in our avoidance, it seems, we often do nothing more than replace one form of violence with another, move the realm of necessity from the world of nature to the world of technique.

31. Ibid.
32. Ibid.
33. Ibid., 99.
34. Ibid., 118.
35. Ibid.
36. Ellul, *Violence*, 127.

With great and constant and unavoidably violent force, our technological culture promises to protect us from violence and consistently delivers on that promise. All we have to do in return is to allow ourselves to be constrained, limited, shaped, and guided by values that aren't our own; to give up everything that makes us most authentically human—our curiosity and creativity, our empathy and reason, our organic connections to nature and to each other. True human freedom is found in that brief, too-frequently comfortable interval between the stimulus and the response, between the offer and the acceptance, and in the realization that freedom is that perpetual struggle against necessity implicit in our conscious free will.

References

Adorjan, Michael, et al. *Stockholm Syndrome as Vernacular Resource.* The Sociological Quarterly 53 (2012) 454–74.

Ellul, Jacques. *The Presence of the Kingdom.* Second Edition. Colorado Springs: Helmers & Howard, 1989.

———. *Propaganda: The Formation of Men's Attitudes.* Translated by Konrad Kellen and Jean Lerner. New York: Vintage, 1965.

———. *The Technological Society.* Translated by John Wilkerson. New York: Vintage, 1964.

———. *Violence; Reflections from a Christian Perspective.* Translated by Cecelia Gaul Kings. New York: Seabury, 1969.

Ferguson, Brian. "Pinker's List: Exaggerating Prehistoric War Mortality." In *War, Peace, and Human Nature: The Convergence of Evolutionary and Cultural Views*, edited by Douglas P. Fry, 112–32. Oxford; Oxford University Press, 2013.

Frankl, Victor. *Man's Search for Meaning.* New York: Touchstone, 1984.

Frey, Rebecca J. "Stockholm Syndrome." In *The Gale Encyclopedia of Medicine*, edited by L. J. Fundukian, 4134–36. Detroit: Gale, 2011.

Keeley, Lawrence H. *War Before Civilization: The Myth of the Peaceful Savage.* Oxford: Oxford University Press, 1996.

Namnyak M. et al. "'Stockholm syndrome': psychiatric diagnosis or urban myth?" *Acta Psychiatrica Scandinavica* 117 (2008) 4–11.

Oxford English Dictionary. 2nd ed. 20 vols. Oxford: Oxford University Press, 1989.

Pinker, Steven. *The Blank Slate: The Modern Denial of Human Nature.* London: Penguin, 2002.

Strentz, Thomas. "The Stockholm Syndrome: Law Enforcement Policy and Ego Defenses of the Hostage." *Annals of the New York Academy of Sciences* 347 (1980) 137–50. Online: http://biodiversitylibrary.org/page/35448487.

Chapter 10

Technology and Perpetual War: The Boundary of No Boundary

David Lovekin

IN THE NOVEL *1984*, George Orwell described a society engaged in perpetual war, where citizens believed slogans that proclaimed war was peace, that ignorance was strength, and that freedom was slavery. Contradictions were not contradictions. This was accomplished for the outer and inner parties through a control of language—Newspeak—where oppositions could not be expressed and, therefore, not thought; members of the outer party were under constant surveillance and were encouraged to spy on each other. The "proles" were left largely on their own, controlled by manufactured poverty and scarcity, by drunkenness and gambling, and by other forms of self-delusion and indulgence.

Mostly the real year 1984 came and, for many, went with few serious warnings. There was no Big Brother; Oceana, Eastasia, and Eurasia did not exist; democracies seemed to flourish and there was much to buy and sell. There is currently much concern about governmental spying, about physical and psychological torture of prisoners of war, and about maintaining control over terrorism, however that is configured. Mostly, there is no concern about advancing technology, except in specific instances like environmental safety, or concern about the trivializations of communication and language. The internet is praised for making knowledge—a proliferation of facts—available. Facts produce knowledge; technology is power; and freedom is proper control, organization, and efficiency. And yet, there is increasing violence and war, however named. Politicians lie with impunity—in their terms they "misspeak." News organizations make claims regardless of truth value of which few seem to care or to be aware, content with the "power to change the channel." Democracy seems to have become the right to vote—although under attack—for choices offered and carefully managed to serve the interests of those with power and money. Corporations, the Supreme Court has ruled, are people. But, for some there is indeed much to bring worry.

Jacques Ellul was a great prophet for these concerns. In his view technology enslaved both thought and language, co-opting choice. Violence, he held, was the subjugation of a populace to an order of necessity that was endemic to the state that was created by violence and then sustained by it. War is organized violence, called "force" when enacted by the state. Ellul did not believe this attempt at legitimation held; violence was violence.[1] Ellul wrote:

> Necessity appears when Adam breaks his relation with God. Then he becomes subject to an order of obligation, the order of toil, hunger, passions, struggle against nature, etc., from which there is no appeal. At that moment necessity becomes part of the order of nature—not of nature as God wished it to be, but of nature henceforth made for death. And death is then the most total of necessities. Necessity is definable as what man does because he cannot do otherwise.[2]

Ellul offers five laws or aspects of violence that appear in all cultures at all times: continuity, reciprocity, identity or sameness, bi-reciprocity (violence engenders violence, as he states it), and hypocrisy as in the need for self-justification.[3] These aspects are controversial like many of Ellul's lists.[4] There are many useful accounts of these aspects, but I offer my own with my concern for violence and the dialectic as it wrestles with necessity and with a sense of absolute limits. By dialectic I will mean the relationship between consciousness and the object of that consciousness such that the object appears as an "other" to that consciousness. Important in this relationship is the opposition of the "other" that remains. For human knowl-

---

1. Ellul, *Violence*, 84–92.

2. Ibid., 128.

3. Ibid., 93–108.

4. See Goddard, *Living the Word, Resisting the World*, 167–98. Goddard sorts through many distinctions and potential problems.

edge the object is always an "other," even in the awareness of that relation. Reality and its truth is always beyond what is known and what is claimed. The "other" provides a limit and thus a condition for further knowlegedge. Pride, by definition, is canceled in this aspect. Violence typically occurs in hubris, in an apparent certainty that denies the truth or the importance of the "other." The aspects of violence also resonate with what Ellul has called the characterology of the technical phenomenon and with the limits of language as found in the symbol and the cliché.

Violence is a madness, a fury, a form of hubris which proceeds without limits.[5] These notions are behind the five aspects that suggest a continuum of discord, a lack of self-awareness and control but are certainly behind continuity, which denies the aspect of the "other."[6] The dialectic is canceled for Ellul with the "other" denied. Violence becomes a closed circle with the other—group or individual—suppressed.[7] Sameness or identity involves a cancelling of difference, either psychologically or physically, if these can be separated in matters like economic exploitation. Once engendered, all bets are off. Torturing begun will spread everywhere regardless of governmental, social, or cultural differences. Each side of a disagreement will claim brutality for the other side.[8]

What I have called bi-reciprocity is merely a continuation of the first three aspects with a difference in emphasis in a loss of objectivity and therefore subjectivity. Death is welcome to revolutionaries who challenge oppression. Machinegun fire and war cries mingle. Ellul asks: "Who said that—Hitler or Che Guevara? No one can tell."[9] Violence in its fourth aspect suggests some awareness of wrong, of hatred unleashed, in as much as there are calls for justification.[10] Each side needs to justify its violence. Propaganda and the clichés of nationalism or group identity or self-interest will serve the ends of justification.

As I will show, the dialectic as ground for self-knowledge and freedom is at risk in the loss of self -control and awareness this violence brings. Will self-knowledge end violence? If it is simply a part of the human's fallen state, the answer would seem no. But, if there is no ontological fault, if self

5. Ellul, *Violence,* 98.

6. Ibid., 94.

7. Ibid. 96.

8. Ibid., 99.

9. Ibid., 103.

10. Ibid., 104.

-knowledge can somehow align with an absolute, with a partly wholly other, another condition may be possible. I will discuss this later. I now move to considering the various forms of necessity facing self-knowledge in the city, in language and the symbol, and in the prospects for absolute knowledge.

Part I

The city is both a metaphor and a literal place for Ellul. The motivation for the city occurs after Adam's break with God that results in painful labor and toiling; Adam no longer cultivates God's perfection already given.[11] In Eden, Adam was allowed to participate in the naming of the animals with their true names, a naming that ends with Adam's break. Eve did not have a name prior to this but then is named, suggesting a confusion of powers.[12] Humanity decides to make a language for itself.[13] The human city, beginning with Babel, becomes the place of technique, violence and murder; humanity is separated from nature mind and body, displaying a finitude and a confusion in language. Increasingly humanity comes to live in opposition with God, with true nature, and with humanity itself.

Ellul's writing moves in sociological, theological, and philosophical dimensions that never stray far from culture and history subject to interpretation. His critique of technology runs parallel to a symbolic interpretation of the Bible that is supported by a theory of the symbol and language. Humanity loses its freedom from the moment it decides to take and make the world in its own terms in a bid for freedom based on technology that is a mentality that forgets that it is finite and limited, a knowledge embedded in the city. God made the human free, while the human opts for a necessity and an enslavement that seems free. The real that humanity helps to make must be understood as just that—a making that portends perfection based on mathematics-like methods reaching for an absolute of efficiency that is either finite or empty and failed. To confuse this real with the true, the finite with the infinite, is to make free choice impossible. The human does violence to itself and embraces a dehumanization and alienation thought to be liberating. To choose requires that the terms of choice be understood. Freedom requires a dialectical understanding in which the other is a fundamental aspect of experience. The other is what I am not and is the basis

11. Ellul, "From the Bible to a History of Non-work," 43.
12. Ellul, *Humiliation of the Word*, 66.
13. Ellul, *Meaning of the City*, 19.

on which choice is made. The tension between myself and what I am not but would choose to be supplies the grounds of language, society, and individuality. I will develop these ideas and explain these tensions more fully.

In considering language Ellul noted the fundamental importance of tension and contradiction between form and content, between what is said and what is meant. Without that tension there is no language and meaning. Ellul wrote:

> . . . tension or contradiction is based on a similarity between signifier and the thing signified (when that tension disappears, there is no more language—that is why, whatever one may think, imagined reproduction of reality is not language); the other aspect is the tension between two interlocutors: if a difference does not exit, if they are identical, there would be no language because it would have no content; if a common measure did not exist, there would be no language because if would have no form.[14]

Language requires the other in what Ellul calls a dialectical tension. Language after the Fall is essential to human culture. He wrote, "Tension between groups composing the entire society is a condition for life itself, or life susceptible to creation and adaptation in that society. It is the point of departure for all culture. There is no necessary dialectic. The possibility of this dialectic movement is the condition for life in societies."[15]

Thus cultures and societies require tension because absolute knowledge is not human knowledge in which idea and object, word and meaning, individual and group are separated. By attempting to silence difference and to obtain an abstract objectivity, individual freedom and creativity are violated. Relations between groups are likewise compromised. False necessities are confused with real necessities; false agreements made by clichés and propaganda subvert the real necessity for dialogue and dialectic that produces a creative opposition fueled in a tension between image and word, the real and the true, the is and is not. Freedom is messy from the standpoint of technique. The possibilities of violence and war are thus, by definition, by the necessity of tension, around every corner.

But the possibility of freedom is given granting God's gifts of symbolic meaning and the hope of life after death and of the possibility of a True that defines the real or the apparent. God, for Ellul, is no empty universal but is a perfection that submitted to imperfection and embodiment, a life

14. Ellul, *Political Illusion*, 215.
15. Ibid., 217.

in Jesus Christ documented in the gospels. The Bible gives Ellul the faith and understanding provided by the symbol in which what is and is not are not separated. God is no simple identity but is a part in all of his creation, a participant as it were in all life. One of course could say that God is life and that all of life ultimately finds its meaning in this totality if one knew how to find the whole in the part. Or that God is the ultimate meaning obtained both outside and inside the part of which this meaning would constitute a whole. One could say that God is the life that is after any death in which even the dying and dead participate. But this might grant too much for a conservative Ellulian, whomever that may be. Nevertheless in my reading of Ellul the technical phenomenon and the technical operation, language (both meaning and meant) and the symbol and the symbolized should stand in tensions where one does not collapse into the other. I hold that a form of meaning that transcends these relationships without being reduced to them or without becoming an empty universal is required. Later I will hold that this problem was anticipated in Hegel's discussion of the bad or spurious infinity and that his remarks are helpful to any thinker working on the notion of God. I will also suggest adding a more sophisticated reading of Hegel's dialectical approach that Ellul anticipates and which does not result in any false synthesis or, indeed, in any syntheses at all.

Violence, for Ellul, is a condition of the fallen world that can, nonetheless, be met by symbolic readings and responses that do not necessarily lead to war or to mindless tortures and humiliations. This would be part of the Christian's duty. I think it should be part of the human's duty. An otherness that transcends the day to day, that is judgmental but forgiving, that is loving and creative and life affirming should start to do the job. In *The Presence of the Kingdom* Ellul wrote:

Concretely, we see that unless the world can re-discover, by a spiritual revolution, an end which is both transcendent and present, an end whose presence can be perceived even in the secret world of technics, it is lost.[16]

The very idea of the symbol partially meets these conditions. The symbol explains a series and is not simply a part, like n+1. This is certainly symbol like. The counting numbers are infinite and n+1 includes them but also transcends them in meaning. The liberal arts thrive on symbols. Symbols require interpretation. It may be no accident that much world conflict today is largely between the monotheisms of Christianity, Judaism, and Islam, certainly conflicts in symbology. It may also be no accident that

16. Ellul, *Presence of the Kingdom*, 89.

these conflicts are also largely matters of technology's incursions into the world order.

Part II

The necessity of technology is the subject of *The Technological Society*. The technical phenomenon is produced out of a dialectical relation of the technical operation on a natural object or process. The tool—in an operation—extends from the body to create, change, or force. Technical consciousness intervenes in this process in search of the one best way with the goal of absolute efficiency. *La technique* is a mentality not to be confused with its constructs like machines although seen as deeply connected. The object is reified, conceptualized, and the technical phenomenon is the result.[17] The phenomenon proliferates such that technical choice, aping a mathematics-like method, is made automatically in all areas. Technical rationality is employed like the laws of logic. A equals A. A cannot be both A and not A. But, in lived experience as in technical productivity, this abstraction does not hold. The moment I think of A, A thought of is different than the first A, the-A-not- reflected-upon. Writing it down is no help. One A is to the right; the other is to the left. For this reason, productivity increases such that, for example, the absolutely perfect soap appears endlessly, always in the next moment. That is why the soap isle in supermarkets is so full. Technical choice is made automatically, Ellul noted. Four is always greater that two. In warfare, poison gas must always be fought by poison gas or worse. That which can be done will be done. Choices are endlessly made but always in terms of technique, which, in the logic above, always denies difference and contradiction, although contradictions abound in this process.[18] They are simply ignored or denied. Coke becomes the real thing among numerous incarnations and imitations. In the end the phenomenon becomes the perfected natural object—in some cases may be named a natural imitation—and is the new sacred; it is that which must be and which alone is deserving of respect.[19] The dialectic between subject and object collapses

17. Ellul, *Technological Society*, 19–22. For a full discussion of technical consciousness see Lovekin, *Technique, Discourse, and Consciousness*, 82–116.

18. See my discussion of technological logic in Lovekin, *Technique, Discourse, and Consciousness*, 58–176.

19. Ellul, *Technological Society*, 61–147. See also Lovekin, *Technique, Discourse, and Consciousness*, 157–87.

when consciousness no longer stands before the object in opposition as an other. Ellul understood that the dialectic kept choices open. It became clear in considering the aspects of violence above that the character of monism—what can be done will be done—summarizes the aspects. It also become clear that as subjectivity and objectivity collapse in the technical process a sacred order appears that is self-justifying and therefore morality denying. Anything goes.

Clichés and propaganda create and fortify the necessity of the state that supports technology and the violence it engenders by ridding language of meaning and tension, the concerns of *Propaganda*,[20] *The Political Illusion,* and *The Critique of the New Commonplaces.*[21] The illusion of politics is that politics is necessary even when it no longer exists. *Le politique,* where goals and values supporting the general good of the community are debated, discussed, and enacted, succumbs to *la politique,* the methods, practices, techniques of implementation.[22] *La politique* is *la technique.* Language, Ellul concludes, displays the importance of a fundamental tension both of form and content, meaning and meant as mentioned earlier. He also considered the tension between groups as the starting point of all cultures, the product of a cultural dialectic mirrored in language where meaning always exceeds the grasp. With the cliché one means only what one says, which cancels interpretation, debate, and discourse. Symbols become signs. A stop sign only means stop unless a poet gets hold of it and makes it sing. Again the dialectic stops. Truth is eliminated in fact. As above, *la politique* and *le politique* are no longer in tension. The cliché is the linguistic version of the technical phenomenon, the machine in a new suit and a version of an embodied concept. The origins of technical phenomenon are usually unknown. Who could recall that a cliché was once a printer's dab? Now the cliché is more than merely a tired expression.[23] Orwell would have been proud. Ellul typically centers his critique in his theological and sociological by addressing the cliché. For example, in *Violence,* he cites the clichés that material gains are the most important gains and that happiness is socially governed. Then he concludes with:

20. See Ellul, *Propaganda.*

21. See Ellul, *A Critique of the New Commonplaces.*

22. Ellul, *Political Illusion,* 3 n. 1.

23. See my discussion of the cliché in *Lovekin, Technique, Discourse, and Consciousness,* 201.

humanity finally comes of age with the advancement of technology.[24] There is no meaning, no opposition behind these terms. One might as well say, "Technology is: hallelujah" and be done with it.

In *The Meaning of the City*, Ellul showed the city as a challenge to God that marked a break with God, with absolute meaning. God gave humanity freedom while humanity opts for orders of human necessity. Meaning becomes relative and languages babble. Babel is the incarnation of this incoherence. The city begins with Abel's death. The separation from God heralds the resultant fragmentation of community and language.

They all have one language. And they have undertaken to make a name for themselves. A humanity capable of communicating has in its possession the most terrible weapon of its own death: it is capable of creating a unique truth, believed by all, independent of God. By the confusion of tongues, by non-communication, God keeps man from forming a truth valid for all men. Henceforth, man's truth will only be partial and contested.[25]

Genesis provides the myths that contain and explain the facts. Humans are finite and imperfect and so is their making. Babel meant "confusion," Ellul noted, but it also means so much more, how symbols in biblical myths work. He wrote,

> When I use the word [myth] I mean: the addition of theological significance to a fact which in itself, as an historical (or supposed to be such), psychological or human fact which in itself, has no such significance. Its role is therefore to make a fact "meaningful," to show it up as bearing the revelation of God, whereas in its materiality it is neither meaningful nor of the nature of revelation. This is how myth operates. It does not destroy the historical reality of the event, but on the contrary gives it its full dimensions.[26]

The symbol is the key to the door beyond technical necessity. Ellul wrote,

> Man cannot have a relationship with another save by the intermediary of symbolization. Without mediating symbols, he would invariably be destroyed by raw physical contact alone. The 'other' is always the enemy, the menace. The 'other' represents an invasion of the personal world, unless, or until, the relationship is normalized through symbolization. Very concretely, to speak the same

24. Ellul, *Violence,* 35–43.
25. Ellul, *Meaning of the City,* 19.
26. Ibid., 18 n. 3.

language is to recognize the 'other' has entered into the common interpretive universe. . . .[27]

The enemy is thus symbolized and brought into a common world, however much that world can be disrupted. He wrote, "I have demonstrated that the aristocracy in primitive Rome could not have emerged except by the process of symbolization."[28] This was held against the claim that the aristocracy appeared by and through force. Great deeds were made into an account, which gave meaning to their actions instead of destroying the meaning of others.

God's deeds are recounted biblically: God is what is; God is a God of sacrifice—He gave himself as Jesus; he is a God of judgment; he is a God of love. The Bible is narrative of contradictions between which meaning occurs. How can self-sacrifice be love? How can judgment be forgiveness and salvation? How can God be both Three and One?

God never justifies violence although humans are not kept from it. They are to learn from it, Ellul would say. Violence in the Bible is shown to be contradictory and confrontational but not necessarily meaningful. As Ellul often noted, dialectical confrontation brings forth meaning; violence that is non dialectical is cacophony. For example, at the root of human experience is the tension between the image and the word. The image is what appears before me; it is what it is—a mere appearance in the realm of the visual. It is singular, spatial, and non-contradictory. I cannot see a mountain as both a mountain and not a mountain; I can say the mountain is not a mountain but is the place where major conflicts lurking behind modernity occur, especially if I am Thomas Mann and then one of his attentive readers. I can do this with the word. I can see that God appears behind biblical events recounted in the Bible but I cannot see Him. The image is in the realm of the Real, *le Réel*, and the True, *le Vrai* abides in the realm of the word. Ellul's reading of biblical texts attempts to move from the image to the word—from the sign, the signal, to the metaphor. The true becomes the whole in the dimension that surrounds. God's perfection locates human finitude, defines it, and is behind the human attempt to achieve it, and Ellul finds this in biblical revelation but also in human experience, history, and institutions. This is a dialectic that wars against necessity and against war and violence.

27. Ellul, "Symbolic Function, Technology, and Society," 210.
28. Ibid., 212.

The word, any word, is never the object or the image. Images and the awareness of them never combine but are always separate, and the awareness of this builds meaning not separation. Building in the realm of the city is endless. Ellul wrote, "When men no longer understand themselves, the city which was the seal of their understanding loses all meaning for them. And henceforth it will always be so. Men can live in their towers, they can build their skyscrapers and their giant cities, they can cover the world with a web of interlocking cities, but these have no more meaning for them. Babel will never be finished."[29]

Even the internet does not complete the city. Human words attempt to imitate the Word, but they should do so knowingly. Any finite word, certainly Ellul's words, suggests meaning that is beyond what I grasp and which I seek from all the regions possible. I know move to more dialectical matters.

Part III

I never meant to say that Ellul was a philosopher but only that my interests in him were philosophical, not claiming my love of wisdom to be wisdom itself.[30] Like Hegel and Ellul I believe that the true is the whole, the totality of what can be meaningfully said and thought about anything. In this sense, I am a liberal artist and try to profit from what all the disciplines can teach. I do not regard Ellul merely as a sociologist or as a theologian, not because he said that he wasn't, but because his reading and thinking mount the entire range of the humanities. I have said that I thought Hegel's notion of the dialectic is useful in getting to Ellul's point and adds a useful dimension, although my reading of Hegel is likely different from Ellul's. A common

29. Ibid.

30. See *Lovekin, Technique, Discourse, and Consciousness,* 10–12 and 24–25. Van Vleet, *Dialectical Theology and Jacques Ellul,* 28 is close to my reading but errs when he claims that I stated Ellul's dialectic is "informed primarily by Hegel." There are of course other influences: Kierkegaard, Barth, even Weber, but I offer Hegel's dialectic as I read it to further Ellul's cause, not to reaffirm Hegel's. Also, Andrew Goddard claims I'm too busy with my philosophical interests to note that Ellul was a sociologist (see Goddard, *Living the Word,* 137). I would never dispute the obvious. My point is that Ellul is much more than a sociologist, even a sociologist of Georg Simmel's stripe. My reading is philosophical and I think the more readings the merrier. To narrow a perspective on Ellul is to do violence to it. I have never said that Ellul was primarily a philosopher, to dispute Goddard's claim. But, I am a philosopher of culture with an emphasis in the history of ideas, if I have to limit myself.

misreading of Hegel is that he thought in terms of thesis, antithesis, and synthesis.[31] He did not. He never used these terms. In *The Phenomenology of Spirit* (the basis of my reading) Hegel displayed the dialectic in two moments: there is awareness and then an awareness of that awareness and the two never coincide, although they appear to do so, perhaps want to do so.[32] The famous master servant example illuminates. I am no master and serve a master's interests, but to know this is to understand that the master depends upon me. While not the master, I am not the same kind of servant knowing that the master depends on me.[33] Even more simply I can note: I am cold but not aware that I am; aware that I am, I put on a coat. More to the current point, to be a soldier is to be ready to kill, but to know this is to raise the question of why, how, when, etc.? What are the limits of my awareness and the awareness of awareness and of the boundaries that surround? Would I kill and under what circumstances? What would constitute the necessities? Where does freedom lie? Whatever I appear to be, I am also something else from the standpoint of a second awareness. This is, at core, where human freedom lies, and I take this to be Ellul's point. I apply tools to make devices; I make bodily motions to program a computer; I consider the possibilities of my actions using scales and charts. But, I am none of these things, processes, concerns, totally. But, my actions, whatever their nature, their time and place, their results and implications, have meaning. That meaning should also be my concern, but it is Ellul's point that this is no longer the case. These choices not known are not made and in these way we are slaves to what we have made that now make us; and this ignorance often comes back to bite us, to issue in violence on a grand scale or a local small scale. In either case, the dehumanizing process that takes the human out of the range of responsibility is the problem. Here Ellul locates the problem of violence in a wide ranging way that is disturbing to many of his more literal minded readers.

Hegel noted that in attempting to form a notion of the infinite, two problems occur.[34] One problem is to reduce the infinite to one member of the class that the infinite defines or represents. This makes the infinite just

---

31. Verene, *Hegel's Recollection*, 18–19. Verene's book was essential to my understanding and interpretation of Hegel.

32. Hegel, *The Phenomenology of Spirit*, 46–57 and 79–103. Also see Verene, *Hegel's Recollection*, 14–26.

33. Ibid., 114–19. Hegel's terms are "lord" and "bondsman."

34. Ibid., 139–210. What Hegel calls "the unhappy consciousness" is unable to deal with the two forms of awareness that never become one.

one more moment and as a boundary is useless. This is certainly the case in productivity, in the march of the technical phenomenon. It is certainly a problem for biblical interpretation that tries to reduce God's being to one moment, to one aspect of a story—for example to the God of judgment and to the God of forgiveness. The Trinity, of course, is a familiar conundrum to the literal minded. The other problem is to say the infinite is simply outside the class denoted and connoted. This infinite has no parts, has no real relation to what it claims to define or represent. This would be a God held to be merely unknowable, leaving the problem of how that can be known to worthier or weaker intellects. These problems constitute what Hegel calls the bad or spurious infinity.[35]

Part IV

In this paper, I have examined Ellul's views of violence and war as an extension of technology's mentality. Technology has defined reality that people have come to live, which may be a concentration camp with no suffering.[36] Pleasure and happiness are coterminous with high living standards and with material wellbeing. Values are now material and available at hand, often determined by whim and availability, both of which are declared by advertising and other various forms of propaganda appearing as the "news." One is no longer free, Ellul claims, to not choose from the cornucopia of technique and this exacts a violence, a dehumanization, on the populace. The debate over total war is useless because, "the means are totalitarian," regardless of the form of government in play.[37] This dehumanization is heightened by clichés and other "humiliations" of the word where symbols are no longer viable, where meaning and meant are on different planes. Meaning is reduced to the visible, which makes meaning problematic and creates a void, which for some is replaced by war and conflict.

Chris Hedges, in *War Is a Force that Gives Us Meaning*, documents his fascination with the wars that he experienced as a journalist from the Balkans to the Persian Gulf. War fills a spiritual void, Hedges noted, like love that involves camaraderie, commitment, and sacrifice. Wars evoke covenants that do not erupt because humans cannot agree out of an inherent

---

35. Hegel, *Hegel's Science of Logic*, 138–51. See my further discussion of this in Lovekin, *Technique, Discourse, and Consciousness,* 98–105.

36. Ellul, *Technological Society,* 103.

37. Ibid., 285.

bellicosity but instead appear in agreements between participants and goals. However, covenants in war, ". . . lack an adequate sense of humility and an acknowledgement of the sinfulness of our own cause . . ."[38] making them false covenants and lacking in objectivity. The object disappears in a strange absorption in this lack of objectivity. In war nothing is given in return, unlike being in love; war, instead, is like a narcotic.[39] Hedges concludes, "War finds its meaning in death."[40] The negativity of war is masked in propaganda and endless attempts at justification: the world will be a better place; we are making the world safe for democracy; we are fighting an endless war on terrorism. Wars, in fact, have become "extended military engagements."

Enemies on all sides are objectified, turned into objects. The names are well known although not often acknowledged. "Profiling" occurs in airports, on the subway and in the street, and with those enforcing the law—soldiers, the police, the vigilantes—apply the same techniques—the reduction of the person or group to the image. Hedges notes, "Each side creates a narrative. . . . Only one message is acceptable."[41] The story is clearly important and symbols are staged but all are denuded in clichés.

There is a strangely aesthetic dimension to war that Hedges (with a biblical nod) calls a "lust for the eye."[42] Few Americans will forget the 2003 night of televised fireworks as Baghdad was revealed in "Shock and Awe." If it was missed, there are a plethora of YouTube videos of it. War is impossible, Hedges states, without a certain kind of fundamentalism, a certainty that the gods, God, Krishna, Allah, etc. is on the believer's side.[43] The irony of destruction is conflated with a perverse sense of renewal and creation. And now I return to Ellul. He describes the aspects of violence clearly in all of the above terms: continuity, reciprocity, sameness and identity, bi-reciprocity, and hypocrisy. These, as well, can be placed over the characteristics of the technical phenomenon that flow from attempts to embody the logical laws of identity and non-contradiction. All of the above are sacrifices of the other—difference—on the Procrustean bed of technique. The cliché replaces the symbol and language and communication are trivialized.

38. Hedges, *War Is a Force that Gives Us Meaning*, 162.

39. Ibid.

40. Ibid., 144.

41. Ibid., 73.

42. Ibid., 89.

43. Ibid., 147.

Ellul is clear that meaning has to transcend the meant. The whole must be wholly greater than the part, but the whole must also appear in the part or, perhaps, make the part appear in the whole. The Jesus story for Ellul is a chronicle of failed hubris as Jesus confronts corruption and alienation, ideologies hardened on stone tablets, bureaucracy and social determinisms. Jesus is both God and human, and this paradox drives Ellul's sense of meaning in which God appears backlit in the biblical narrative. There are, of course, other narratives. Krishna appears in the Bhagavad Gita as both whole and part, armed with paradoxes that suggest a just waging of war that is ultimately futile. Robert Oppenheimer turned to the Gita on July 16, 1945, as prelude to testing the A- bomb, where Krishna appears as death and as the destroyer of worlds. The bomb was tested in any case. For me, Ellul's accounts of technology, biblical literature, the history of philosophy, and the philosophy of history—in short, the totality of the liberal arts— keep me returning to a quest for wholeness that leaves out none of the parts and yet a quest that is rooted in history, literature, institutions, the things and ideas and stories that humans have made. Even Christianity for me becomes a part of the whole, but I do not want to fight over it.

References

Ellul, Jacques. *A Critique of the New Commonplaces*. Translated by Helen Weaver. New York: Knopf, 1968.

———. "From the Bible to a History of Non-work." Edited by Carl Mitcham. Translated by David Lovekin. *Cross Currents* 35 (1985) 43–8.

———. *The Humiliation of the Word*. Translated by Joyce Main Hanks. Grand Rapids: Eerdmans, 1985.

———. *The Meaning of the City*. Translated by Denis Pardee. Grand Rapids: Eerdmans, 1970.

———. *The Political Illusion*. Translated by Konrad Kellen. New York: Knopf, 1967.

———. *Presence of the Kingdom*. Translated by Olive Wyon. New York: Seabury, 1967.

———. *Propaganda*. Translated by Konrad Kellen & Jean Lerner. New York: Alfred A. Knopf, 1965.

———. *The Technological Society*. Translated by John Wilkerson. New York: Vintage, 1964.

———. "Symbolic Function, Technology, and Society." *Journal of Social and Biological Structures* 3 (1978) 207–18.

———. *Violence: Reflections from a Christian Perspective*. Translated by Cecilia Gaul Kings. New York: Seabury, 1969.

Goddard, Andrew. *Living the Word, Resisting the World*. Carlisle, PA: Paternoster, 2002.

Hedges, Chris. *War Is a Force that Gives Us Meaning*. New York: Public Affairs, 2002.

Hegel, Friedrich. *Hegel's Science of Logic.* Translated by A. V. Miller. London: Allen & Unwin, 1969.

———. *The Phenomenology of Spirit.* Translated by A. V. Miller. Oxford: Clarendon, 1977.

Lovekin, David. *Technique, Discourse, and Consciousness: An Introduction to the Philosophy of Jaques Ellul.* Bethlehem, PA: Lehigh University Press, 1991.

Van Vleet, Jacob E. *Dialectical Theology and Jacques Ellul: An Introductory Exposition* Minneapolis, MN: Fortress, 2014.

Verene, Donald Phillip. *Hegel's Recollection: A Study of Images in the Phenomenology of Spirit.* Albany, NY: State University of New York Press, 1985.

Chapter 11

My Conversion to Christian Pacifism: Reading Jacques Ellul in War-Ravaged Central America

Mark D. Baker

"Good Guys and Bad Guys"

GROWING UP IN THE 1960s, my favorite television shows were "Combat" and westerns. Along with a steady stream of cowboy and Indian movies I watched many Second World War movies. All of these programs clearly distinguished "the good guys" from "the bad guys." These films facilitated my viewing issues, causes, and nations in a simplistic way. As I looked at the world and read history I saw countries and movements neatly separated in two categories, "good guys" and "bad guys."

The same television that displayed John Wayne triumphing over the Japanese brought me the news from Southeast Asia. The former influenced the way I thought about the latter. Just as John Wayne always played the "good guy," I assumed the US and those who fought with us were the "good guys." Just as John Wayne always won, I expected the US to win. As a grade-schooler I had little grasp of the issues behind the fighting. I knew that the communists were the "bad guys." I assumed that the same was true in Viet Nam as I had been taught about other wars, the US had to fight to protect democracy and freedom.

The Vietnam War did not offer the fronts and invasions of the wars I saw on TV movies. Looking at a map did not give me a sense of who was winning. Hence, body counts acted as my gauge of the war's progress. The evening news would show a little chart that separated the "good guys" and the "bad guys" into two columns and listed the number of casualties. We almost always "won" this war of numbers. In my young mind it seemed just a matter of time before the other side would run out of soldiers and lose.

Things did not happen as I envisioned it. A war that was going on when I started grade school continued to grind on as I moved into junior high. I did not understand why we did not win. It confused me that we did not just go over there and bomb them until they gave up. By the time US troops left Vietnam, I, like most, was glad to not have to see it on the news every night. In 1975 South Vietnam fell, and I graduated from high school. I left for college still unaware of the complexity of the issues surrounding the war I had grown up with. The Vietnam War had only forced me to recognize that "good guys" do not always win.

I want to make a parenthetical observation here about TV. I watched a lot of TV as a child, including a lot of war movies, westerns, and other violent programs. It did not, however, turn me into a murderer, or a violent person. So one could use me as an example to say TV is not so bad, or so powerful. But the reality is that TV was a very powerful shaping influence in my life. It helped form my world view, a world view that neatly distinguished between right and wrong, and put me and my country firmly on the good side of that line of distinction. Television fostered within me a belief in the myth of redemptive violence. It portrayed violent force as a tool, either a tool for good or for evil. The difference was the goal. Good people used force for noble goals. Thus TV contributed to me having an "ends justify the means" approach to life. Television helped me come to closely link my country, patriotism and my faith.

My Neatly Categorized View of the World Crumbles

In college my clear-cut way of dividing causes into categories of good and bad moderated. Through history courses I came to see that the same event can be interpreted in different ways, and that a nation can have a variety of motivations in foreign and domestic policy. Even so, when I graduated and moved to Honduras in 1979 I basically continued to evaluate things from a black and white, "good guys and bad guys" perspective.

I did not go to Central America for political reasons. I had the choice of teaching social studies at a mission school in Honduras or one in Peru. After four years of Midwest flatness, I opted for the mountains of Honduras over a flat jungle in Peru. I probably did not even know who Anastasio Somoza was. Central American politics, however, quickly became a major topic in my life. Somoza was the military dictator of Nicaragua. His family had come to power with US assistance and had maintained power for decades with US support.

I arrived in Honduras in August, 1979. The Sandinista revolution had triumphed over Somoza in neighboring Nicaragua just the month before. Although concerned about the Sandinista's Marxist tendencies, like many, I saw Somoza as the "bad guy." His corrupt dictatorship clearly went against the ideals of freedom and democracy I had grown up with. In 1979 in Central America my world view with neat and clearly defined categories remained.

El Salvador, however, presented a less clear picture. As time went on the situation became harder for me to understand. The guerrillas were openly Marxists. From my perspective that made them the "bad guys," but the army and the Salvadoran government were hard to embrace as the "good guys." Their anti-communist stance and US backing would normally make them the side I would support, but stories of murdered civilians, priests, and nuns confused the issue. Therefore, in 1982 I eagerly accepted the invitation to visit a Salvadoran refugee camp in Honduras. I hoped that talking to Salvadorans would help me more clearly understand which side was right in El Salvador.

As I helped the refugees construct more permanent shelter I asked them why they had fled El Salvador. Every person I asked said they fled because of the army. Many told me how soldiers had killed their neighbors, including the elderly, women, and children. Others explained how the army had invaded a town on the other side of a hill from their own. Some sadly recounted that even though their family escaped from the army's attack of their village they had lost children or relatives by drowning or from machine guns shot from helicopters as they attempted to cross the river in to Honduras. Whether they had firsthand experience or were fleeing so that they would not, all feared the army. I had expected people to have different opinions on which side they supported in the war. I planned on sorting through the various opinions to put together my own conclusion. No sorting was needed. They all said basically the same thing. I did not talk to anyone who tried to persuade me that the guerrillas were the "good guys," but they all indicated that the army was their problem.

My simple view of the world, and its neat categories, exploded on an August Saturday afternoon in that dusty refugee camp. I asked a middle-aged woman, as I had others, why she had fled. She replied, "The army killed my seventeen-year-old son." I did not press for details, but she continued talking. As tears ran down her face, she told me how the soldiers had dragged him from the house, cut off his hands and feet and shot him through the head. Voices argued within me. The logical orderly world view of my youth led me to think: "there must have been a reason they did that." Scrambling for some way to understand I found myself saying, "Perhaps they thought your son was a guerrilla." She replied, "I have never seen a guerrilla, they never came into our village." Suddenly, war, which had made so much sense when John Wayne did the fighting, became disgusting, destructive, and tragic. I had written a paper on the "just war theory" while in college, but emotionally I became a pacifist in that refugee camp.

In a college class I had heard a panel of four people present their views on whether Christians should participate in the military. One of the presenters was Howard Claassen, a physics professor and one of two Anabaptist faculty at the college. We had to write a paper in response and I argued for just war theory. I did not write with a lot of conviction, but I also did not write with a lot of doubt. It was the position that made sense with the world I had grown up in—a world where flags were in the churches I attended, where Christian friends and relatives served in the armed forces, and television shaped my world view.

In truth I really did not have a Christian position on war and violence. In churches I grew up in we did not even engage the issue. I don't recall ever talking about it in Sunday school or youth group. Like the rest of the country we just followed our leaders in to one military action after another without ever discussing whether the actions fulfilled the requirements of the just war theory we supposedly embraced. If, rather than just hearing a lecture and writing one paper, I had been a part of discussions about the just war theory, then perhaps on that August afternoon I would have responded differently. In my anger and horror I might have said, "This killing of unarmed non-combatants is not just. This is therefore not a just war and Christians must refuse to participate and protest the injustices our tax money is supporting." Just war theory, however, was not in my thoughts that day.

While living in Honduras I had met a number of Mennonites. It was actually through friendship with a Mennonite Central Committee worker that I went to the refugee camp. I knew their position on pacifism and non-resistance, and I became more aware than I had in college that there was a very strong biblical case for pacifism. But in a certain sense it remained fairly academic until that hot sunny afternoon in the refugee camp.

I had seen the evil fruits of war in the faces of these people and I did not like it. In my gut I had converted to pacifism. Intellectually, however, I was confused. Pragmatically, pacifism did not make sense, how can you expect a nation to not have an army and not use force? My visit convinced me that the Salvadoran government and army certainly were not the "good guys," but what about the guerrillas? Besides my deep-seated negative feelings about communism, I was also a student of history and economics. I knew that what the revolution offered, more economic equality in El Salvador, was certainly needed; yet I also knew that historically communists had not produced what they espouse. So, even though my disgust with the army made me want to support the guerrillas, I could not. I did not see them as the "good guys" either.

I returned to my home in Tegucigalpa with these questions churning in my mind. A later trip to El Salvador itself, when I actually walked through villages that had been attacked and burned, would only confirm my thoughts. In a sense the trip to the refugee camp cleared up the picture for me. It did not, however, allow me to analyze the situation in the simple and clear way I had wanted. When people asked me what I thought of El Salvador I found myself saying: "Both sides are wrong, the violence is wrong, it is a mess." This answer bothered me. I felt the need to say: "This side is right and we should support them." My position felt like a cop-out.

Reading Ellul's Thoughts on Violence

Soon after this trip to the refugee camp, while looking at the bookshelf of a missionary from whom I borrowed books, the title *Violence: Reflections from a Christian Perspective* jumped out at me. I noticed that the author was Jacques Ellul. Another missionary friend, Bob Ekblad, had enthusiastically recommended Ellul to me. I had looked at the Ellul books Bob had and borrowed and read the one that appeared the lightest reading, *Prayer and Modern Man*. Now, however, Bob's recommendation of the author, and my pressing questions, made the book on violence the choice that day.

I expected a book, like others I had seen, that picked one position, pacifism, or just war theory, and selected Bible verses that supported its position and ignored or explained away passages against its position. Ellul's book, however, surprised me. It differed from any I had seen on the topic. He did not exactly fit into either of the positions I was familiar with—at least as I understood them.

Ellul: Traditional Christian Approaches to Violence

Ellul begins *Violence* by explaining and evaluating three traditional Christian approaches to violence. He first summarizes what over time became the "just war theory." This stance accepts that the State has the right to use force, and saw the church's role as determining whether the State used force justly or not. Theologians developed a list of seven conditions that must be in order for a war to be considered just:

> the cause fought for must itself be just; the purpose of the warring power must remain just while hostilities go on; war must be truly the last resort, all peaceful means having been exhausted; the methods employed during the war to vanquish the foe must themselves be just; the benefits the war can reasonably be expected to bring for humanity must be greater than the evils provoked by the war itself; victory must be assured; the peace concluded at the end of the war must be just and of such nature as to prevent a new war.[1]

Ellul acknowledges that these conditions have theoretical solidity. He questions, however, if we can apply them in our age of modern warfare with the same certainty they were applied in the Middle Ages. He also questions the underlying assumption that humans can control violence and keep it in the service of order and justice.

In conclusion Ellul calls this position a solution of compromise. He supposes the reasoning behind it ran something like this: "We certainly have to live in society. These are no longer the days of the first Christian generation, when extreme uncompromising attitudes were possible. We must accommodate ourselves to the situation that exists; we must become part of it if we are to go on living."[2]

---

1. Ellul, *Violence*, 6.
2. Ibid., 9.

He next addresses the nonviolent position which goes back to the beginnings of the church. In fact it appears to have been the dominant position in the early church, with most Christians refusing to serve in the army until the fourth century. There are two common versions today: One approach to nonviolence centers on the person. "It is in being himself at peace that a man becomes peaceful; it is in living the love of God that he becomes capable of manifesting that love; it is through his practice of it in his personal life that nonviolence spreads to society."[3] The second approach centers on the military and its growing power. It recognizes that an oppressive or unjust government can remain in power only because of the armed force it has behind it. Therefore, the aim of nonviolence is this: "the state must be divested of its instruments of violence; and, for their part, proponents of nonviolence must respond to the state's use of violence by nonviolent actions."[4] Gandhi is heralded as an example of this position put in practice, but Ellul questions whether Gandhi would have had the same success in all situations, in Russia in 1925 or Germany in 1933? He also questions the assumption that a government can maintain itself without ever using violence. (And, as we will see in a moment, in relation to the first Ellul is critical of those who see this as a strategy for making society non-violent.)

The third position, which like the first two has a long history, is Christians for violence. Some hermits of the Nile valley during the third and fourth centuries first carried out this idea. They went into cities, beating up people and smashing everything in sight. "They took it upon themselves to punish sinners here and now and to manifest God's judgment on the world in concrete ways."[5] Since then, however, Christians have more commonly supported violence when they see it as a means to liberate the oppressed. Often this position uses Christianity to justify or legitimize revolutionary or political actions. (Bombing abortion clinics or killing doctors who perform abortions would be a contemporary North American example of this category.) Although firmly committed to helping the suffering, they willingly inflict violence on others and cause them to suffer.

Ellul concludes by saying that all three positions are alike in the respect that they all insist upon a Christian "solution," a valid way of organizing society. (Although that does not always have to be the case with the first

3. Ibid., 13.
4. Ibid., 14.
5. Ibid., 17.

aspect of the second position above.) They attempt to formulate a compromise between the demands of Christ and the necessities of the world. They want to reorganize society along Christian lines, but have forgotten that this world has absolutely rejected Jesus Christ. Ellul believes that "we are invited to take part in a dialectic, to be in the world but not of it, and thus seek out a particular, a specifically Christian position."[6] He sets out to do this in the rest of the book.

Ellul: Laws of Violence

Ellul first desires to take a realistic look at violence, seeing the facts as they are and grasping them thoroughly. As a Christian, Ellul has an advantage over others in attempting this task. Terrible as the reality may be, he can analyze the reality without despairing because of his hope in Jesus Christ. Ellul bases his realistic look at violence on study and experience. He states that he has on several occasions participated in movements that used violence, including the Spanish Civil War, and the French Resistance during the Second World War.[7]

He begins his appraisal by pointing out "that every state is founded on violence and cannot maintain itself save by and through violence."[8] Violence is universal, and it is also of the order of Necessity. "I do not say violence is a necessity, but rather that a man (or a group) subject to the order of Necessity follows the given trends, be these emotional, structural, sociological, or economic. He ceases to be an independent, initiating agent; he is part of a system in which nothing has weight or meaning; and so far as he obeys these inescapable compulsions he is no longer a moral being."[9]

Ellul concludes that violence is inevitable. He then turns to the consequences of violence, and outlines five laws of violence.

6. Ibid., 26.
7. Ellul, *Perspectives on Our Age*, 18.
8. Ellul, *Violence*, 84.
9. Ibid., 91.

The First Law of Violence is Continuity

Once you start using violence you will continue to use it. Violence is easier and more practical than other methods, dialogue for instance. Revolutions born in violence set up a reign of violence for a generation or two.

The Second Law of Violence is Reciprocity

Here Ellul borrows Jesus' words from Matthew 26:52 and writes that all who live by the sword will die by the sword. Jesus makes no distinction between good and bad use of the sword. All "violence creates violence, begets violence and procreates violence."[10]

The Third Law of Violence is Sameness

In this law Ellul is not evaluating the reasons violence is used, and saying you can't make any distinction between better and worse reasons for using violence. Rather he is writing about the violent act itself. If you are shot by "justified violence" or "unjustified" it feels the same, has same affect. Whether a bomb is detonated for justified reasons or as an act of terror the explosion and destruction are the same. In that sense that you cannot distinguish between justified violence and unjustified violence. Ellul is not saying the purposes for using violence are the same, rather he seeks to lead us to recognize that even if we may have good reasons to justify use of violence, it is still violent.

Ellul also maintains that we should not try to differentiate between physical violence and economic violence or psychological violence. "The velvet-glove violence of the powerful who maintain the regimes of injustice, exploitation profiteering, and hatred has its exact counterpart in the iron-fist violence of the oppressed."[11] Violence is the same also in the sense that you cannot in reality put limits on it. If you condone violence it is impossible to say "So far and no further." We have seen the impossibility of setting up laws of warfare, or we can imagine the impossibility of putting limits on torture. "The man who starts torturing necessarily goes to the limit; for if he decides to torture in order to get information, that information is very important; and if, having used a 'reasonable' kind of torture, he does not

10. Ibid., 95.

11. Ibid., 98.

get the information he wants, what then? He will use worse torture."[12] An implication of the sameness of violence is that if we use violence ourselves we have to consent to our adversary using it. A government that maintains itself by violence cannot protest when others use violence against it. In the same way, rioters or revolutionaries often seem to think that all the "rights" are on their side, they complain about police brutality, but what about their own brutality?

The Fourth Law of Violence is That Violence Begets Violence—Nothing Else.

People say we have a good goal, but unfortunately we have to use violence to achieve it, but it does not happen. Mao or Castro did not bring justice. As Ellul said, "Violence can never realize a noble aim . . . evil means corrupt good ends. But I repeat also: 'Let the man who wants to use violence, do so; let him know what he is doing.' That is all the Christian can ask of this man."[13]

At first glance this appears to be an Ellulian overstatement, and there might be some of that. But I think we should focus on the "corrupting." He is not saying that violent force doesn't change things, and to some degree "accomplish" things, but as Martin Luther King Jr. said:

> Through violence you may murder a murderer, but you can't murder murder.
>
> Through violence you may murder a liar, but you can't establish truth.
>
> Through violence you may murder a hater, but you can't murder hate.
>
> Darkness cannot put out darkness. Only light can do that.[14]

Violence is expedient, it changes things, but it is not a solution in the profound sense. The power (using the word in the sense of *echthroi*, "principalities and powers") embodied in militarism tells us the opposite—that violence can be redemptive. It tells us that more bombs and bullets will bring more control. It deceives us into thinking we are solving a problem when we use force, or that we have no other option, but to use force.

12. Ibid.
13. Ibid., 102.
14. King, "Where Do We Go from Here?"

The Fifth Law of Violence is That Those Who Use it Try to Justify Violence and Themselves.

I could see the truth of Ellul's laws in history. I thought that I would not say them quite as strongly as he did, yet in essence I agreed with him. (As I continued to read other Ellul books I discovered how much he likes to make extreme statements, and I later understood why he makes them.) What troubled me most, however, at this point in his book, were the implications of what he had written. On one hand he states that violence is of the order of Necessity and inevitable, on the other hand he takes a very negative view toward violence and what it will accomplish. I had come to the book with doubts about the pacifist position of some Christians because it did not seem feasible. Can you really expect a country to not have an army or police force, to not use violence? In a sense I found Ellul's position even more confusing because he did not deny that a country would have to use force, yet he takes a negative position towards using force. Looking back I can now see that I was having my first encounter with Ellul's dialectical thinking. Naturally this clashed with my traditional black and white, either or, way of looking at the world. "Combat" and John Wayne did not present a dialectical view of violence.

Ellul: The Fight of Faith

Although no less dialectical, Ellul's next chapter, "The Fight of Faith," answered the questions he had left me with. He answered one question I had by explaining that although a Christian should remind the State that they are responsible to God she cannot demand that the State not use violence—that would be suicide for the State. "Christians must not require others to act as if they were Christians . . . If an ethic is Christian, it is a product of the faith." To demand that non-Christians live by this ethic would be to set up objectives they can neither understand nor obtain.[15] The role of the Christian is to try to limit the effects and remedy the causes of violence. "But we shall not be able to deter men from violence."[16] We should marvel, when peace breaks out.

Ellul explains that unfortunately Christians make the mistake of accepting that which is necessary and inevitable as legitimate. "This is

15. Ellul, *Violence*, 159–60.

16. Ibid., 158.

anti-Christian reasoning par excellence. What Christ does for us is above all to make us free . . . to have true freedom is to escape necessity or, rather, to be free to struggle against necessity. Therefore I say that only one line of action is open to the Christian who is free in Christ. He must struggle against violence precisely because, apart from Christ, violence is the form that human relations normally and necessarily take."[17] So, just as Ellul acknowledges that we cannot expect the State to behave in a Christian way free from Necessity, he demands the opposite of Christians. "The better we understand that violence is necessary, indispensable, inevitable, the better shall we be able to reject and oppose it. If we are free in Jesus Christ, we shall reject violence precisely because violence is necessary."[18]

Christians must always side with the oppressed—often violence will seem the easiest way to help them—but Ellul states that "the appeal to and use of violence in Christian action increase in exact proportion to the decrease in faith."[19] The main duty of the Christian today is to act as a mediator, to plead the cause of the oppressed before the powerful. At times the Christian may find him or herself working with people who are involved in a violent struggle, but she must never condone their violence. In fact, the Christian should try to help them see their violence in a realistic light.

To show that her action was not ideological a Christian must switch sides if the oppressed become the oppressors. Ellul cites his own experience in France during the Second World War. At the end of the war, the oppressors–traitors during the war—became the persecuted. At that point the Christian should have switched from attempting to mediate for the Resistance to attempting to protect the persecuted from the now victorious Resistance.

Because violence is of the realm of necessity in this world there will always be the temptation for the Christian to use violence as a last resort. In conclusion, however, Ellul states that for the Christian the true last resort is prayer, resort to God. In a situation of violence this may prove much more difficult than taking up arms. For instance, Ellul wrote this book when the Black Power movement in the United States was on the rise. He writes:

> How is it that, in the midst of the racial struggle going on in the United States today, so many white Christians leave to black Christians the appanage of nonviolence? Why do they not take

17. Ibid., 127.
18. Ibid., 130.
19. Ibid., 149.

the way of repentance and conciliation in the face of black violence—repentance for the violence the whites committed in the
past? Why, in the face of the black violence they provoked, do
they not now seek 'peace at any price'? It is only by love that is
total, without defense, without reservation, love that does not cal-
culate or bargain, that the white Christian will overcome the evil
of revolution, arson, and looting. . . Neither exaltation of power
nor the search for vengeance will ever solve any human situation.
In accepting death, Jesus Christ showed us the only possible way.
We may refuse to take it. But we must realize that when we refuse
we are left with one alternative—increasing the sum of evil in the
world. And we ought to be honest and renounce all pretensions to
the Christian faith.[20]

To some this may seem an escape. Ellul admits that some will say that
Christians are absent from the world because they refuse to participate in
the necessity of violence, but he ends his book with these words:

Will it be said that Christians are absent from the world? Curious
that "presence in the world," should mean accepting the world's
ways, means, objectives; should mean helping hate and evil to pro-
liferate! Christians will be sufficiently and completely present in
the world if they suffer with those who suffer, if they seek out with
those sufferers the one way of salvation, if they bear witness before
God and man to the consequences of injustice and the proclamation of love.[21]

Where Ellul Brought Me

I had left the refugee camp with conflicting perspectives. My gut told me
both sides in the conflict were wrong. My head, which was still operating
from a, good-guy and bad-guy mindset, told me that it was intellectually
unacceptable to not support one side or the other. My head told me I was
copping out by criticizing both sides. Furthermore, my gut told me violence
was wrong, my head told me that was not a realistic position.

Ellul's book connected with what my gut told me, and it convinced
my head that as a Christian this was an intellectually acceptable position.

20. Ibid., 174.
21. Ibid., 175.

A year earlier I would have had trouble understanding Ellul's message; four years earlier I would not have even given him a chance.

My trip to the refugee camp brought my black and white world view crumbling down because I could not fit the things I heard there into a clear and neat, right-wrong framework. Reading *Violence* by Ellul helped me see the weaknesses of my former way of viewing things. For instance a "good guys—bad guys" world view very easily leads to an "ends justify the means" attitude. Deciding that someone else was bad allowed me to think that anything we, the good guys, did to stop them was acceptable. My own experience helped me see that the good guys and bad guys cannot be so neatly divided. Ellul showed me the danger of thinking the ends can justify the means. In fact he demonstrated that the means affect the end. Corrupt means, like violence, corrupt the desired end. Ellul also opened up a whole new way of approaching issues. Before I had pragmatically looked at what options the world had to offer and tried as a Christian to select the best one. Ellul challenged me to look deeper and to go beyond what the world offered.

References

Ellul, Jacques. *Perspectives on Our Age: Jacques Ellul Speaks on His Life and Work*. Edited by Willem H. Vanderburg, Toronto: House of Anansi, 2004.

———. *Violence; Reflections from a Christian Perspective*. Translated by Cecelia Gaul Kings. New York: Seabury, 1969.

King, Dr. Martin L. "Where Do We Go from Here?" annual report delivered at the 11th convention of the Southern Christian Leadership Conference, August 16, 1967, Atlanta, GA.

Appendix

Book Reviews

THE FOLLOWING TWO BOOK reviews are included to provide readers with a look at two of Ellul's more important books that deal with violence and revolution. Numerous other book reviews can be found in the archives of the *Ellul Forum* at the website https://journals.wheaton.edu/index.php/ellul. Readers are encouraged to submit an article or suggest a book for review to the forum so that the active engagement with Ellul's thought can continue.

Autopsy of Revolution
Andy Alexis-Baker[1]

In this book Ellul delves into history arguing that until the eighteenth century, revolt had been conservative and opposed to political and social change. These upheavals revolted against unbearable situation resulting from increased state functions. As such, revolution (or revolt) reacted *against* the expected course of history and usually wanted to restore a previous situation.

Then came the French Revolution which changed traditional revolt in two ways: a future oriented outlook and belief in the state as the bearer of freedom. The aristocratic leaders envisioned a utopian society which a scientific outlook would bring about. Inspired by the French Revolution, Karl Marx made revolution part of history's evolution. Thus revolution became normalized and predictable. All that were needed were the right

1. This review appeared in the *Ellul Forum* 38 (2006).

techniques to predict the conditions under which the masses would explode and to direct the explosions into seizing control of the state, which under the direction of new management would take on a totally new character: communist.

Ellul argues that in reality the state has its own internal logic and structure so that those who think they can control the state are under an illusion, instead that logic and structure controls the revolutionary. Revolution, rather than decreasing state power, has increased the state's reach. The dehumanizing, rationalized gaze of the state has penetrated into every area of life. It is state power, more than colonialism or class-conflict that truly threatens human freedom. Here Ellul becomes relentless in his attack on every aspect of the nation-state.

Ellul suggests that the alternative to state fetishism is a revolution invoking "direct personal responsibility."[2] Much contemporary discourse is still based upon the notion that where real "politics" of action occurs is in the impersonal machinery in Paris or Washington DC. Ellul, however, insists that the only real thing is the person—spiritual, physical and mental. Call it anarchism, personalism or situationism, (Ellul uses all these terms while recognizing differences), the idea is the same. Real change happens where people begin to take responsibility. For Ellul, modern electoral democracy attempts to tame the inherent anarchy and unruliness contained in democracy.

Ellul does not call for traditional individualism. He makes clear how statism and the technological society *create* individuals who are incapable of making decisions that run against nationalist or technological ends. Yet because of his polemic against a herd mentality, he fails to make clear that rootedness and loyalty to a certain type of community helps individuals become whole persons, without which the lures of the technological society quickly overwhelm. For me—a Mennonite—Ellul's failure to place individuals in community is inexcusable. The state is primarily about creating individuals without attachment to healthy community and loyalties that make it possible to fight the technological society. At times Ellul seems to forget that while the great Fascist and Communist regimes depended upon massive public support, our own democracies depend upon mass apathy and individualization.

Despite the failure to name types of community that resist state expansion and the technological society, this book is valuable for *Ellul Forum*

2. Ellul *Autopsy,* 282.

readers to re-read. The dominant emphasis for the *Ellul Forum* has been the pitfalls of the technological society. Yet Ellul insists, "Any revolution against the perils and the bondage of technological society applies an attempt to disassemble the state."[3]

Ellul's claim that the state is the object of revolution is also true for advocates of nonviolent techniques. Gene Sharp and others tout the great "nonviolent revolutions," but using Ellul's outlines it is best to point out that this is just another vulgarization of the word. No revolution has occurred in any Western nation since Ellul's book. What happened were in-house regime changes. No Western "revolution" has successfully dismantled that state and the technological apparatus (the Zapatistas in Chiapas, however, come closer to Ellul's vision).

Finally, if a future edition of this book were printed, it would benefit from a critical apparatus and an index. Ellul mentions and discusses numerous names, places and movements that North American readers may not understand without editorial footnotes. Despite these flaws in the apparatus of the book, the content remains relevant for those of us concerned about the expected course of history. Ellul's call is for revolt against this dark future looming over us. And it remains as dark as Ellul ever predicted it would be.

References

Ellul, Jacques *Autopsy of Revolution*. New York: Knopf, 1971.

3. Ellul, *Autopsy*, 268.

The Political Illusion

Randal Marlin[4]

Forty years ago Konrad Kellen gave the American public a fine translation of *The Political Illusion*, along with an insightful introduction. This work builds upon Ellul's earlier *Technological Society* and *Propaganda*. A central question here is: How can a conscientious citizen in a modern democracy contribute to good government? Those with technical expertise can be expected to look out for their own special interests, not necessarily the public good. Withstanding corruption requires proper checks and balances. But this requires the appropriate knowledge, and who will supply that?

Ellul commonly devotes the bulk of his energies, in his social and political writings, to trenchant diagnosis of social problems. He points the way to solutions, but is careful above all not to encourage complacency. He sounds the alarm, saying in effect: beware the fancy imagery of democracy, behind which the mechanisms of tyranny may be crafted.

Passage of time has shown Ellul to be prescient. Certainly in the United States the Watergate debacle, the Iran-Contra dealings, and the current deceptions of the administration of President George W. Bush to bring his country and a coalition into war with Iraq, followed by use of torture and rights violations of detainees, surveillance of US citizens without court authority, and the like, all reinforce the main claims in this book.

Central among these claims is the idea that uncritical faith in democratic processes, such as the party system and elections, to provide us with good government, is misplaced. The idea that such processes will guarantee democracy is undermined by awareness that votes are valuable only to the extent voters are informed. Once it becomes clear that government, technocrats and co-operative media shape the information and imagery reaching the public, the idea that the ordinary voters are the real determinants of political power becomes very dubious.

Upton Sinclair and, more recently, Noam Chomsky have presented us with similar insights, but Ellul goes further in locating the problems as having their source in popular attitudes and in the dominance of myths concerning progress, happiness, and the ability of the right technique to solve our problems.

The true source of democracy, for Ellul, lies in the attitudes of the people. "A personal conscience," he writes, ". . . is the only thing that can

4. This review appeared in the *Ellul Forum* 38 (2006).

save both democracy and what is real in political affairs."[5] Enemies of democracy can be found even among those who profess to favor it. These enemies are fanaticism on one side, and inertia, leading to opting out of politics, on the other. You can't have genuine democracy without a deep-set respect for the opinions and aspirations of others, including minorities within the larger society.

The idea that happiness will be guaranteed if only we can get people to adjust and adapt to majority views, and if we can maximize material comforts, is one of those myths than emboldens political powers to intrude in the private sphere to encourage uniformity. Ellul refers here to Bernard Charbonneau (to whom he dedicates this book) and what Charbonneau calls the "lie of liberty," namely, liberty conceived as offered to the individual on a platter by a benevolent society. By contrast, "There is no liberty except liberty achieved in the face of some constraint or rule."[6] The aptness of the Saint-Just quotation at the front of the book makes itself felt here: "The people will fancy an appearance of freedom; illusion will be their native land."

Among the many wry observations about Bush's failed (as is currently acknowledged even by original supporters) Iraq war is that the supposed exporters of democracy were simultaneously undermining it at home. The recent November election switched the congressional power from Republicans to Democrats, but it remains to be seen whether much can now be done to reverse the beginnings of civil war there. What good is an election when the die, in the form of a quagmire, has already been cast?

Ellul thinks that unity in a political system means that life has gone out of it. Tension and conflict form personality, "not only on the loftiest, most personal plane, but also on the collective plane." I see a resemblance to Emmanuel Levinas and the latter's perception that the goal of ataraxy conflicts with the obligation to respect the otherness of the other. To avoid disturbances to our tranquility we would like to make others the same as ourselves. But one only has to look at Canadian history and the effect of Lord Durham's goal of assimilating the French Canadians to see what enduring resentments this attitude can cause.

Ellul is conscious of writing largely from the experience of France since Louis XIV, but he need not apologize for thinking his ideas might have larger application. Centralizing forces exist the world over, and they

5. Ellul, *Political Illusion*, 204.

6. Ibid., 211.

need to be kept in check. He thinks it important to permit the emergence of social, political, intellectual, artistic, religious and other groups, totally independent of the state, "yet capable of opposing it, able to reject its pressures as well as its controls and even its gifts."[7]

He thinks these organizations and associations should be able to deny that "the nation is the supreme value and that the state is the incarnation of the nation." He allows that there is a risk in reducing the central power but sees this as "the condition of life."

Ellul wrote before the arrival of the Internet. We have seen that the ability of the centralized powers in the United States to shape opinion by false imagery failed spectacularly in the attempts to make war heroes out of Jessica Lynch and Pat Tillman - the latter former professional football star having been in fact a victim of "friendly fire." Contrary credible evidence circulating through Web sites such as Truthout, Common Dreams, PRWatch and the like was sufficient to force the image-makers to backtrack.

But there is no guarantee that the freedom exercised by those Web site operators will continue indefinitely, and we can expect battles in this area as well as on other fronts, such as the attempts to force television stations that show government video news releases to acknowledge their provenance in a way that will minimize their deceptive propensities.

The trouble with illusions is that they are comforting, and if our vision of life is to maximize comfort, why bother attacking them? One reason is that illusions can lead to political mistakes which can have most uncomfortable outcomes. Another reason, though, is that other goals and conditions of a good life include such things as such as honesty, freedom, integrity, and respect for the Other, and these are incompatible with the pertinent illusions.

We have to be willing to engage in political life and work for our desired goals, but always in such a way as to preserve our respect for the freedom and dignity of others, even when our goals collide. "We should forever be concerned with the means used by the state, the politicians, our group, ourselves."[8] We also have to track down those stereotypes and myths in our own thinking so as to free ourselves from them, for as long as they exist "no freedom or democratic creativity is possible."[9] Coming from Ellul,

7. Ibid., 222.
8. Ibid., 238.
9. Ibid., 240.

the message is not new, but time and events (including dire environmental forecasts) have merely reinforced its urgency.

References

Ellul, Jacques. *The Political Illusion*. New York: Alfred A. Knopf, 1967.

Subjects

Scripture